The Basic Survival guide for the Zombie Apocalypse

ALLEN WOODMAN

THE BASIC SURVIVAL GUIDE FOR THE ZOMBIE APOCALYPSE

ISBN: 9781729393475

The Basic Survival guide for the
Zombie Apocalypse
Premium Press Publications, Allen Woodman.
1st printing Copyright – 2019
Printed in U.S.A. 2019

TABLE OF CONTENTS

YES, I KNOW ZOMBIES AREN'T REAL!

Zombies are fictional creatures usually portrayed as reanimated corpses or virally infected human beings. They are commonly portrayed as cannibalistic in nature.

A zombie apocalypse is a particular scenario within apocalyptic fiction. In a zombie apocalypse, a widespread rise of zombies hostile to human life engages in a general assault on civilization.

THE BASIC SURVIVAL GUIDE FOR THE ZOMBIE APOCALYPSE

In some stories, victims of zombies may become zombies themselves if they are bitten by zombies or if a zombie-creating virus travels by air, sexually, or by water; in others, everyone who dies, whatever the cause, becomes one of the undead.

In some cases, parasitic organisms can cause zombification by killing their hosts and reanimating their corpses, though some argue that this is not a true zombie. In the latter scenario zombies also prey on the living and their bite causes an infection that kills.

In either scenario, this causes the outbreak to become an exponentially growing crisis: the spreading "zombie plague" swamps law enforcement organizations, the military and health care services, leading to the panicked collapse of civil society until only isolated pockets of survivors remain. Basic services such as piped water supplies and electrical power shut down, mainstream mass media cease to broadcast, and the national government of affected countries collapse or goes into hiding. The survivors usually begin scavenging for food, weapons and other supplies in a world reduced to a mostly pre-industrial hostile wilderness. There is usually a 'safe zone' where the non-infected can seek refuge and begin a new era.

So we all know that zombies are not a real thing. (Hopefully). The fact that dead beings cannot come back to life and that they are unable to eat the living, spreading a horrible contagion or plague on the entire planet as we know it and begin an apocalypse for the human remnants as the planet spins helplessly out of control. OR COULD THEY?

On May 18, 2011, the Centers for Disease Control and Prevention (CDC) published an article, *Preparedness 101: Zombie Apocalypse* providing tips on preparing to survive a zombie invasion. The article does not claim an outbreak is likely or imminent, but states: "That's right, I said z-o-m-b-i-e a-p-o-c-a-l-y-p-s-e. You may laugh now, but when it happens you'll be happy you read this...." The CDC goes on to summarize cultural references to a zombie apocalypse. It uses these to underscore the value of laying in stock water, food, medical supplies, and other necessities in preparation for any and all potential disasters, be they hurricanes, earthquakes, tornadoes, floods, or hordes of ravenous brain-devouring undead.

Zombie films generally fall into the horror genre, some cross over into other genres, such as comedy, science fiction, thriller, or romance. Distinct subgenres have evolved, such as the "zombie comedy" or the "zombie apocalypse".

THE BASIC SURVIVAL GUIDE FOR THE ZOMBIE APOCALYPSE

Zombies are distinct from ghosts, ghouls, mummies, Frankenstein's monsters or vampires

In fact, this book and its author realizes the inconceivable reality of flesh-eating pervasive undead walking about creating havoc upon the still human remaining population is unfounded and unwarranted in all of history.

However, one person's disaster is equal to one's ideal apocalypse I guess.

I am an avid fan of the gory and grotesque imagery of the ever-popular zombie-themed films and television shows that have permeated the theaters and our flat screen TVs at home.

Movies like George Romero's "Night of the Living Dead" back in 1968, are most known for what we think of as zombies.

However, the representation of zombies and the spooky stories came along well before that film was even thought of. Victor Halperin's White Zombie was released in 1932 and is often cited as the first zombie film.

The original concept of zombies actually come from Haitian descent in the Caribbean's.

The English word "zombie" is first recorded in 1819, in a history of Brazil by the poet Robert

Southey, in the form of "zombi". The Oxford English Dictionary gives the origin of the word as West African and compares it to the Kongo words nzambi (god) and Zumbi (fetish).

One of the first books to expose Western culture to the concept of the voodoo zombie was The Magic Island by W. B. Seabrook in 1929. This is the sensationalized account of a narrator who encounters voodoo cults in Haiti and their resurrected thralls. Time claimed that the book "introduced 'zombie' into U.S. speech".

Zombies have a complex literary heritage, with antecedents ranging from Richard Matheson and H. P. Lovecraft to Mary Shelley's Frankenstein drawing on European folklore of the undead. In 1932, Victor Halperin directed White Zombie, a horror film starring Bela Lugosi. Here zombies are depicted as mindless, unthinking henchmen under the spell of an evil magician. Zombies, often still using this voodoo-inspired rationale, were initially uncommon in cinema, but their appearances continued sporadically through the 1930s to the 1960s, with notable films including I Walked with a Zombie (1943) and Plan 9 from Outer Space (1959).

That's Hollywood Right? Well, maybe and maybe not.

THE BASIC SURVIVAL GUIDE FOR THE ZOMBIE APOCALYPSE

Today, in context we can see real stories and headlines that zombies are real or exist among us. The following stories are real and accounted statements from witnesses and police reports actually filed.

In May 2012. A Miami man, now identified as 31-year-old Rudy Eugene, was shot dead by police when he was discovered naked on the MacArthur Causeway CHEWING the flesh off of another unidentified man, who was later placed in critical condition in the hospital and missing 80% of his face, nose, and mouth!

According to eye-witness reports, a police officer commanded him to stop, and when he didn't, authorities open-fired. And according to Larry Vega, who was present at the time:

"The guy just stood his head up like that, with pieces of flesh in his mouth. And he growled."

Police were forced to shoot him at least SIX times before he finally died

In August 2016, a 19-year-old college student, Austin Harrouf, reportedly stormed away from a restaurant in Jupiter, FL, where he'd been dining with his parents, apparently upset over the slow service there. He then wandered into a neighborhood, where a couple, sat in their garage with the door open, enjoying a quiet evening. Harrouf pulled a switchblade on the couple and stabbed them to death, apparently without provocation. A neighbor attempted to intervene and called 911 but was stabbed by the man as well.

When police arrived, they found Harrouf naked, ripping away chunks of the couple's flesh and eating it. He was also growling, grunting, and making "animal noises." Repeated use of stun guns and a police dog could not sway Harrouf from his "meal," and finally three officers had to pull the man away from the bodies by force.

What makes this case especially strange is that Harrouf, prior to this bizarre crime, was a model student who seemed to have things pretty well figured out. It is reported that he had been hanging out with some of his fraternity brothers prior to joining his parents for dinner, but his toxicology report came back clean. Other test results for synthetic drugs are pending, though officials did say Harrouf showed no other characteristic symptoms associated with substances like flakka or bath salts.

Police were left baffled at Harrouf's behavior. Just what exactly happened to this man to prompt such a gruesome crime?

In October of 2010, was the story of Vince Weiguang Li, who was sitting next to a sleeping passenger, the poor, poor Tim McLean, on a bus when he went full living-dead crazy.

Li savagely attacked McLean and DECAPITATED the guy. He then went to town eating his eyes, ears, nose, and tongue while terrified passengers fled for their lives.

Currently, in a maximum security mental facility, Li later admitted the attack stemmed from him believing that McLean was an alien doomed to kill many. Though why he felt the need to eat said alien, is a mystery that perhaps we don't want to know the answer to.

April of 2011 was this story, a young boy in Brazil in a case that had doctors puzzled. The boy was struggling with a grave case of pneumonia and eventually lost the fight due to respiratory failure. Yet at his funeral, while grieving family members were gathered around, the boy shot straight up, smiling while he looked around at all his stunned family members.

He then asked, "Daddy, can I have some water?" Then just like that he peacefully reclined back into his coffin, as he once again went limp. The boy was raced back to the hospital, were mystified doctors were unable to explain what had happened and declared that he was indeed dead.

Whether or not these stories were stemming from a drug use or a severe misdiagnosis from a physician, the stories were reported and the facts contained therein were accounted as truthful and honest.

The inevitable zombie apocalypse has inspired more products, preparedness guides and designs than we can count, but none of us actually think a zombie apocalypse is possible, right?

Scientists have come out many times and said that it would be impossible for our bodies to walk around after we're dead moaning and craving fresh flesh and brains. I mean, sure, after we're dead a body part might spasm for a moment or something, but that is light years away from how we would imagine ourselves zombified.

I had once read an interesting article from Primer Magazine called 5 Reasons the Zombie Apocalypse Will Never Come to Pass. It was insightful and somewhat convincing, but at the same time, I'll admit that television shows like The Walking Dead almost make it seem so realistic that you might start to wonder. So, maybe a zombie apocalypse is possible after all.

THE BASIC SURVIVAL GUIDE FOR THE ZOMBIE APOCALYPSE

A separate article has been creating quite a stir over the past few years as well. It gives a brief explanation for how zombies could actually exist and are scientifically accurate, sort of.

The thing is, zombies in the sense of dead people coming back to life are not possible. However, very alive people who exhibit a zombie-like state is possible. It would have to be caused by a very specific virus, and that virus would have to enter through our noses since our noses lead to the part of the brain which would have to be affected in order for us to transform into super hungry brain dead beings who don't recognize friends or family.

The concept is frightening for sure. That either a private pharmaceutical company would accidentally release a chemical, drug or agent in to the common air system or a military grade ingredient might spill in to the public water system is farfetched, but the reality just might be scarier than anything we could possibly dream up in fantasy would blow your mind, and then you might think a zombie apocalypse is possible after all.

In a not so long ago article posted by the nationally distributed newspaper USA TODAY, it was discovered that there have been many cases of viruses that had accidentally been let out. In the scathing article released in 2017, USA TODAY reported several cases.

The article stated that the Centers for Disease Control and Prevention, which has faced congressional hearings and secret government sanctions over its sloppy lab safety practices, is keeping secret large swaths of information about dozens of recent incidents involving some of the world's most dangerous bacteria and viruses.

CDC scientists apparently lost a box of deadly and highly-regulated influenza specimens and experienced multiple potential exposures involving viruses and bacteria, according to heavily-redacted laboratory incident reports obtained by USA TODAY. Several reports involve failures of safety equipment. In one, a scientist wearing full-body spacesuit-like gear to protect against lethal, often untreatable viruses like Ebola, had their purified air hose suddenly disconnect — "again" — in one the world's most advanced biosafety level 4 labs.

In another published article back in 2015 released by the GUARDIAN newspaper, another scare was reported.

The article and ABC television both reported that The Pentagon has conceded it accidentally shipped samples of a live bioweapon across nine states and to a US air base in South Korea.

In an extraordinary admission on Wednesday, the Pentagon revealed what it called an "inadvertent transfer of samples containing live Bacillus anthracis", or anthrax, took place at an unspecified time from a US Defense Department laboratory in Dugway, Utah.

Nine unspecified states received samples of the bioweapon, which can be fatal if untreated. One sample was also sent to Osan air base in Pyeongtaek, about 65km south of Seoul.

Colonel Steve Warren, the acting Pentagon press secretary, told reporters on Wednesday that there was "no known risk to the general public" and lab workers possibly exposed to the bio agent have not manifested any indications of infection.

Warren said the lab at Dugway was "working as part of a DOD effort to develop a field-based test to identify biological threats in the environment".

The Pentagon is aiding with a Centers for Disease Control (CDC) investigation, Warren said, and "out of an abundance of caution" stopped additional anthrax shipments from its stockpiles.

Pentagon officials would not say more about when the shipment occurred, who was the official responsible nor how inadvertent it was, given that the shipment appeared from Warren's account to be part of a bioweapon detection initiative.

ABC News reported the states receiving anthrax from the defense department lab are California, Texas, Wisconsin, Tennessee, Maryland, Virginia, Delaware, New Jersey and New York.

Yet again In Horsham, Pennsylvania and surrounding towns in eastern Pennsylvania, and at other sites around the United States, the foams once used routinely in firefighting training at military bases contained polyfluoroalkyl substances or PFAS.

EPA testing between 2013 and 2015 found significant amounts of PFAS in public water supplies in 33 U.S. states.

In a most recent case in New Jersey, an odd case of a viral outbreak with no warning or understandable cause. October 2018, A seventh child died in a viral outbreak at a nursing facility in northern New Jersey. In a statement, the Health Department stated: "The New Jersey Department of Health learned that unfortunately another child who was hospitalized due to adenovirus passed away. The young child's death was the seventh death associated with the outbreak at the Wanaque Center for Nursing and Rehabilitation. The child's death is among 18 confirmed cases of adenovirus among medically fragile children at the facility. The strain of adenovirus seen in this outbreak is associated with communal living arrangements and known to cause severe illness."

A day earlier, state health officials confirmed the outbreak of cases of adenovirus at the center in Haskell in Passaic County.

Adenoviruses usually cause mild illnesses but this outbreak affected medically fragile children with severely compromised immune systems.

An infected person can spread an adenovirus by close personal contact, such as touching or shaking hands, through the air by coughing and sneezing, and by leaving the virus on objects that others then touch, the CDC said.

So the idea of a coming zombie apocalypse is not as farfetched as you might suspect. And if aliens wanted to wreak havoc on our planet and change life as we know it, they could put this virus into the air for us all to sniff up, but that is just crazy talk.

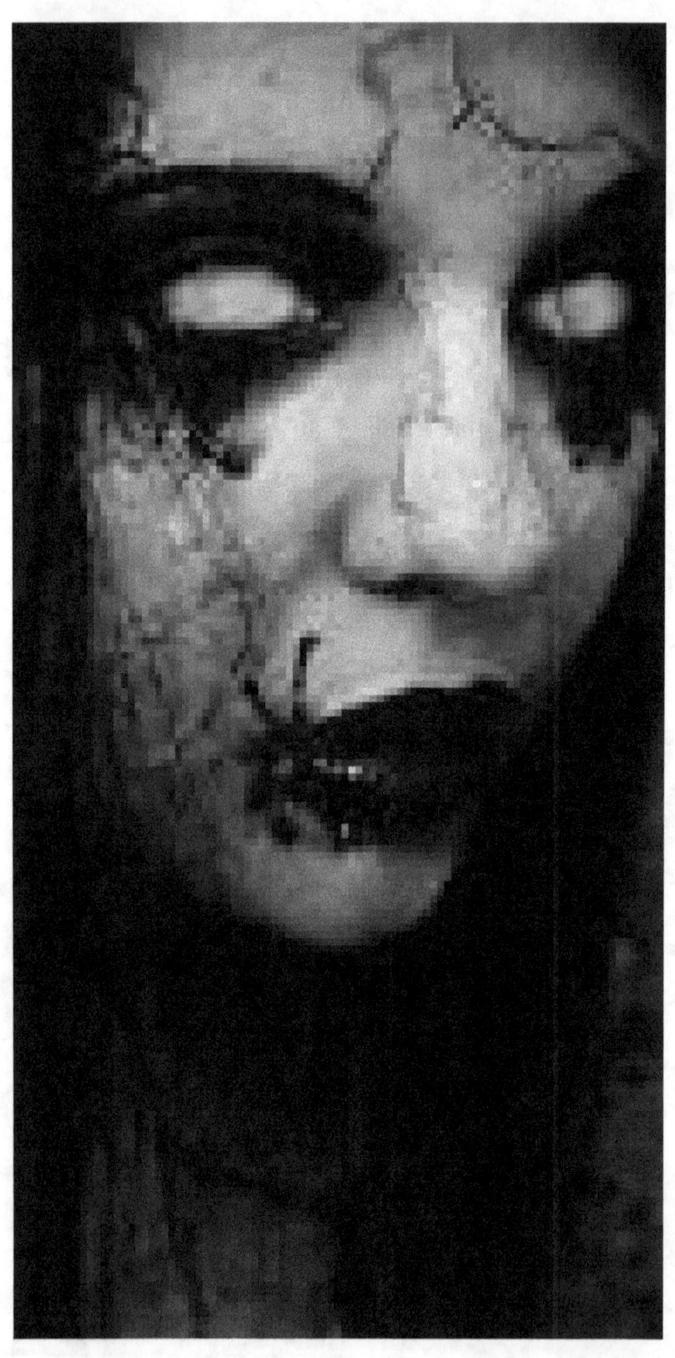

WHAT IF THEY ARE REAL?

I started writing this manual originally as a preparedness guide for those in need of general guidelines for the use in any such disasters that may occur. Hurricanes, Tropical Storms, Earthquakes, Floods or other disasters that may befall the human race at any given time.

The last few years has provided all too many reminders of just how little control man has over nature. Earthquakes have been the disaster du jour of late and we only need only think back to the early 2000's to remember when hurricanes were the biggest scourge to hit the United States. No matter the type of catastrophe, however, being prepared is something that everyone can agree is a valuable goal. The only problem is that it can be a difficult task to prepare for things if you don't know they're coming. Anyone can explore many well-worn paths: seemingly clairvoyant animals, signs from the cosmos, the wisdom of oracles or even computer model to find varying levels of insight of these and others. You can focus on a few key concepts to predate almost any major calamity. Noticing an equilibrium in things around you and your environment can suggests that concentrations of stress are the key indicators of an impending change.

In one case, there are stories of frogs evacuating a vulnerable area before an hurricane hits. Horses and dogs wildly running from an earthquake that doesn't come for hours. Another story, references a point by recounting the tragic irony of the chief executive of Segway Inc. dying by falling off a cliff while riding one of the company's motorized scooters — something that soon transitions into a lesson about the Icelandic volcano eruption last year.

If this all sounds disjointed, it is. But most of the time it actually works. I'm not sure that the ultimate lessons, and thus the reader's actual ability to predict calamities by reading early warning signs, really resonate in interconnected threads, many of which weave together in an engaging, thought-provoking manner.

Here in this one text you will be able to access easily the information to build shelters in various environments, filter water for drinking, find food and how to survive on your own or as part of a team in such case of a disaster or earthbound calamity. This does also account for manmade catastrophes such as nuclear war, viral epidemics or local or national emergencies such as large scale riots or police actions that may infringe upon our constitutional rights of freedom.

With that said, if the apocalyptic event of the walking dead ever does arise you the reader would find useful the technical and practical information given within these pages would help anyone survive.

If that were to ever happen here is what you need to look for to be one of the few survivors of a zombie attack.

THE BASIC SURVIVAL GUIDE FOR THE ZOMBIE APOCALYPSE

The Three Stages of the Zombie Apocalypse

Within this instructional manual any reasonably intelligent person can find the information they need at a glance for full on survival or just enough to get by to help arrives. In the event of an onslaught of dead arising from the grave eating the flesh of humans. You will need to have the necessary skills and learning to help you survive.

There is nothing like being prepared for any such disaster. Having the reliability and readiness of the materials that you and your family will need to rely on should be of primary importance.

Secondly, the knowledge of how to survive in any given situation are skills that one should develop long before any catastrophe arises. Weather it is a Hurricane, earthquake or a horde of walking dead out for flesh. Knowing what to do and where to go is the first step to real survival.

Understanding how the zombie apocalypse will play out is your first step to survival. This is what you can expect.

1. Initial Infection

The first stage of The Walking Plague will be quiet. One person will become infected in a manner we don't yet understand. It could happen in Beijing, China, New Delhi, India or in Tuscaloosa, Mississippi. The virus will either enter their bloodstream through a small cut or it will be airborne. Because the zombie virus takes a little time to transform its host into a lumbering death machine, the host (also known as Patient Zero) will carry the infection around as it replicates inside his or her body. You must be aware at all times. Who touched that doorknob last? Remember your last handshake? Did the guy behind you at Starbucks just sneeze on you?

Patient Zero will spread the virus to others before the virus sheds the host and he or she becomes a full-fledged zombie.

Realistically, you will not ever come into contact with Patient Zero. You might not even know about stage one until it is too late. That's why you should prepare in advance.

2. The Walking Dead

Stage two is when most of us will start to realize there's a problem. Weird pockets of activity will start to make the news, even before the news reports the outbreak itself. You'll know instinctively that the crowd of soccer hooligans turning over cars was moving too slowly. Trust your gut. Being aware will help you react and just may save your life. Things to look for include:

• Unusual activity by pets in your neighborhood. They may be agitated or disappear altogether.

• Someone who gets injured but doesn't bleed.

•A group that slowly engulfs a convenience store and causes damage but doesn't steal anything.

•More than one friend who disappears from social media and real life with no explanation.

• Stepping outside to a sound that is almost like a million cattle mooing – interrupted by the occasional shriek.

•Your neighbors running down the street with pitchforks while other neighbors stumble after them drooling.

• Army helicopters wiping out major metropolitan areas "for the good of us all." Just kidding, that's stage three.

If you start to notice any of these items or other unusual behavior, zombie hordes may not be far behind. The game is on, my friend. Get out of the city while you still can – before The Panic sets in. Before long, traditional media may go off the air, transportation could become permanently obstructed, and power grids might fail.

3. The Long Haul

In stage three, zombies become the new normal. Organizations like the UN and the CDC mobilize on a large scale to fight the virus and protect citizens. That is if the government survives. Have you seen the CDC? It's not exactly armored. And the Secret Service isn't trained for anything of this scale. You will begin to adjust to life in survival mode. It doesn't sound pretty, but if you've made it this far in The Crisis, you have a good chance of surviving long enough to rebuild civilization.

4. Survival skills

These skills are techniques a person may use in a dangerous situation (e.g. natural disasters) to save themselves or others. These techniques are meant to provide basic necessities for human life: water, food, shelter, and habitat, the ability to think straight, to signal for help, to navigate safely, to avoid unpleasant interactions with animals and plants, and cure any present injuries. Survival skills are often basic ideas and abilities that ancient humans have used for thousands of years. Hiking, backpacking, horseback riding, fishing, hunting and many other outdoor activities all require basic wilderness survival skills to handle an emergency situation. Bush craft and primitive living are most often self-implemented but require many of the same skills.

The survivor may need to apply the contents of a first aid kit or, if possessing the required knowledge, naturally occurring medicinal plants, immobilize injured limbs, or even transport incapacitated comrades.

First aid (wilderness first aid in particular) can help a person survive and function with injuries and illnesses that would otherwise kill or incapacitate him/her. Common and dangerous injuries include but are never limited to:

- Bites

- Bone fractures

- Burns

- A headache

- Heart attack

- Hemorrhage

- Hypothermia (too cold) and hyperthermia (too hot)

- Infection through food, animal contact, or drinking non-potable water

- Poisoning from consumption of, or contact with, poisonous plants or poisonous fungi

- Sprains, particularly of the ankle

- Wounds, which may become infected

Take a first aid class to learn precautionary steps to treat yourself and thers for wounds, such as scrapes, cuts, burns and broken bones. First aid classes are usually taught at community centers for free.

Method part 1

How to Treat a Broken Leg

There are several important steps involved in properly treating a broken leg before seeking medical attention. First and foremost, in the event that you suspect a leg broken above the knee, call 911 immediately. Otherwise, continue on with these step-by-step instructions if you suspect a broken leg.

1. Safety first! Make sure the victim is in a safe location. It is more important to worry about rescuers' and the victim's ongoing safety than to worry about the broken leg. Follow universal precautions and wear personal protective equipment if you have it.

2. Control bleeding. If the victim is bleeding from their injuries, take steps to safely control the bleeding.

3. Look for other injuries. If a victim is injured in one area that might be injured in another area. If a victim shows signs of injury to the head, neck, or back, DO NOT move the victim.

4. Cover any broken skin with sterile dressings. If needed, the wound can be rinsed -- try to use sterile water or saline solution.

5. If an ambulance is responding, have the victim remain still and wait for the ambulance. If an ambulance is unavailable, the broken leg may need to be splinted. Be sure to immobilize the joints (knee, ankle, hip) above and below the break. Do not wrap the leg too tight.

6. Put ice on the break to reduce swelling. Put a sheet or towel between the ice and the skin to prevent frostbite. Leave ice on for 15 minutes, then remove ice for 15 minutes.

7. Elevate the leg above the level of the heart, if possible.

8. Lay the victim on his or her back to reduce the chance of shock. Cover the victim with a blanket.

Additional Tips for Treating a Broken Leg

- Remember, DO NOT move a victim with suspected head, neck, or back injuries unless it is to keep rescuers or the victim safe.

- DO NOT move a victim of a broken leg unless necessary for the safety of rescuers or victim.

- DO NOT straighten a broken leg or change its position unless the victim's foot (on the leg with the break) is cold, blue, numb, or paralyzed. Only attempt to return a deformed leg to the anatomical position.

* If splinting the broken leg, try using a broom handle, long wooden spoon, tube from a vacuum cleaner, or a jack handle from the car to stabilize the splint.

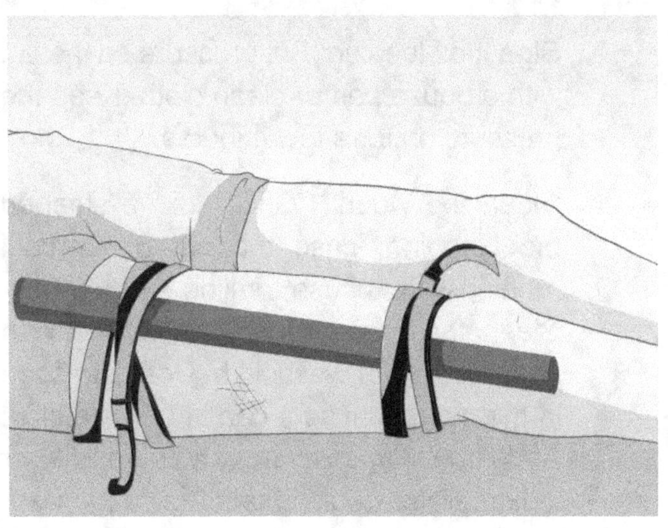

Method part 2
How to Treat a Cut or Scrape

Follow these steps to keep cuts clean and prevent infections and scars.

- Wash your hands. First, wash up with soap and water so you don't get bacteria into the cut and cause an infection. If you're on the go, use hand sanitizer.

- Stop the bleeding. Put pressure on the cut with a gauze pad or clean cloth. Keep the pressure on for a few minutes.

- Clean the wound. Once you've stopped the bleeding, rinse the cut under cool running water or use a saline wound wash. Clean the area around the wound with soap and a wet washcloth. Don't get soap in the cut, because it can irritate the skin. And don't use hydrogen peroxide or iodine, which could irritate the cut.

- Remove any dirt or debris. Use a pair of tweezers cleaned with alcohol to gently pick out any dirt, gravel, glass, or other material in the cut.

Method part 3

How to Treat a Burn

There are a number of ways you can accidentally burn yourself during the zombie apocalypse – whether you spill some boiling water on your hand from a pot or kettle, touch a hot iron, rest against a radiator, or stay out in the sun unprotected too long. These situations can be alarming, but treating these kinds of burns quickly can help extinguish pain and possible scarring.

These types of burns are typically first-degree – meaning you'll have reddened skin and some discomfort, but no blistering. If your skin forms blisters (don't pop those on your own) or develops a "white, leathery appearance" as described by Healthline.com, then you'll probably want to skip the home remedies and go to a hospital. Here are six ways to soothe minor burns without the help of a medical professional (in most of the examples).

1. Cool it Down

Doctors note if you've managed to scald yourself with a hot liquid, then you should run cool tap water over the affected site for at least

10-minutes (up to 20-minutes) – but it specifically says you shouldn't apply ice (although holding a cloth soaked with cool water on the burn will suffice).

If at all possible you should still see a doctor if the burn site includes more than 3-inches of skin, and if it affects your face or certain joints such as the knee, ankle, elbow, as well as the spine and forearms.

2. Pop Some Pain Pills

Often the burning sensation can be a lot to bear for a victim, even in the case of first-degree burns. The Mayo Clinic says almost any over-the-counter painkiller will do – listing ibuprofen (Advil, Motrin), naproxen sodium (Aleve) or acetaminophen (Tylenol) as possible options. Most people will have at least one of these in their home already.

Don't go over the recommended dose on the bottle, even if the pills don't seem to be providing any relief. If you're in extreme pain, then it might be wise to seek emergency help.

3. Apply an Ointment

Once the burn has been sufficiently cooled down, you could add some ointment in the form of petroleum jelly or aloe vera on the affected area. These ointments don't require an antibiotic element, as some of these types of ointments can actually make it worse through an allergic reaction.

Doctors warn against using any creams, lotions, oils, butter, or egg whites on minor burns. Other sources note these can increase the chance of infection, slow the healing process, or aggravate the pain.

4. Protect the Burn

Medical Doctors explain that once you've got the burn soothed with an aloe gel, then you can go ahead and dress the wound to help it heal and protect it from infections. The source suggests using a dry sterile non-stick dressing, which will help prevent it from sticking to the wound if it oozes underneath.

Doing this will also of course help to protect the burn from rubbing against anything directly, which can be painful and open up blisters (if any are present). Be sure to change the bandages every day until the wound is cleared up.

5. Keep an Eye on the Wound

It's important to keep monitoring the burn site for infections. These telltale signs can include increased pain, pus, fever, red streaks extending from the burn site, or even swollen lymph nodes. These symptoms warrant seeking medical attention, it adds.

If you have some of these signs and ignore them, it can take a lot longer for the skin to heal (not to mention you'll have to put up with the unpleasant side effects). It adds that itchiness is not usually a sign of infection – it's a natural occurrence when the skin is healing.

6. Consider a Tetanus Shot

Burns can increase the risk of tetanus, a bacterial infection that can cause serious health complications. Medical experts state that even minor burns can lead to tetanus, so make sure you book a booster shot from your doctor as soon as you can.

Physicians note that bacteria (Clostridium tetani) that can cause tetanus can be found in soil or even dust, entering the body through wounds (typically cuts) and burns.

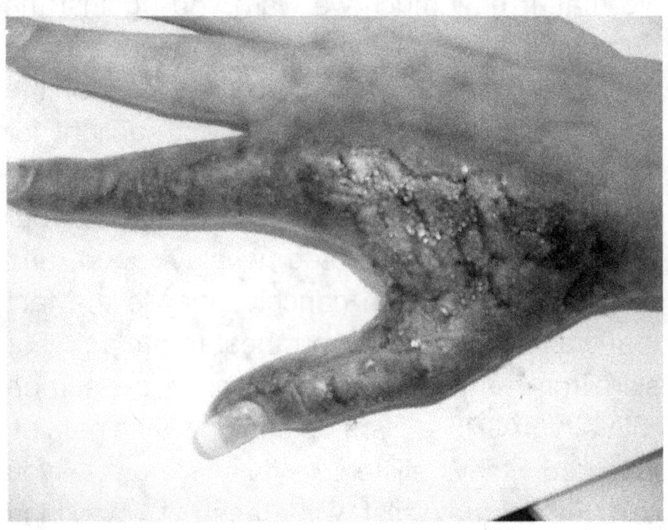

Method part 4
How to Treat a Sunburn

No matter how much we warn you against the damaging effects of UV sun exposure, during the zombie infestation you are likely to be on the run a lot and outside in the direct sunlight for long durations. However, too much sun exposure can cause serious damage to your skin, leaving it dehydrated, wrinkly, aged, and can even cause skin cancer. Despite the fact that we know you'll do your best to protect your skin from sun damage by using a sunscreen with a high SPF—if you do end up with a painful, inflamed, itchy, blistering, flaky sunburn—you can find some relief with these 17 soothing treatments.

1. Oatmeal

Oatmeal is the bomb when it comes to soothing irritated, inflamed skin. It works wonders as a cool compress by wrapping a 1/2 cup of dry oatmeal in gauze, running it under cool water, and applying it directly to your sunburn every few hours.

You know a nice cool shower of bath will cool a fiery sunburn, but lying in cold water might be a bit chilly after a while. Instead, you can apply a cold cloth or a few ice cubes wrapped in a towel directly to the burn. Medical experts advise leaving it on for about five minutes, and reapplying several times a day as needed. The cold compress will help absorb some of the heat from the sunburn, and constrict the blood vessels which in return will reduce swelling.

3. Yogurt

Yogurt isn't just a tasty snack! The natural cultures in yogurt can work wonders on dry skin, so it makes perfect sense that they would also work magic on a stubborn sunburn. Use yogurt as a topical cream and slather it over sunburned areas, leaving it for 5-minutes, then rinse off under a cool shower.

4. Witch Hazel

Witch hazel is a beneficial natural astringent with anti-inflammatory properties, which is why it also soothes painful acne and razor burn. For a sunburn, apply a few drops on a moist cloth or cotton swab and dab directly onto skin.

5. Baking Soda

This might seem surprising, but apparently it works! When cooling off in a lukewarm bath, mix in a couple scoops of baking soda. Dermatologist Fredric Haberman, MD, talked to Prevention and said the baking soda works to help relieve the itching and inflammation, and allow the skin to retain moisture. For the best results let the water (mixed with baking soda) air dry rather than rubbing it with a towel to dry off. This will help make sure the baking soda really soaks in and soothes the pain, and avoid irritating the skin by rubbing a towel against it.

6. Hydrocortisone

An over-the-counter hydrocortisone topical cream, spray, or ointment can soothe inflamed and painful sunburns. Just be sure to look for a topical solution with at least 1-percent hydrocortisone listed in the ingredients. The American Academy of Dermatology advises not to treat with any products that end in "-caine" (i.e. benzocaine) because these will only further irritate the skin and could cause an allergic reaction.

7. Apple Cider Vinegar

It might sound like it would sting, but apple cider vinegar will actually provide the relief you need from sunburn. Just add a cup to your bath water or apply it like an astringent with a cotton swab.

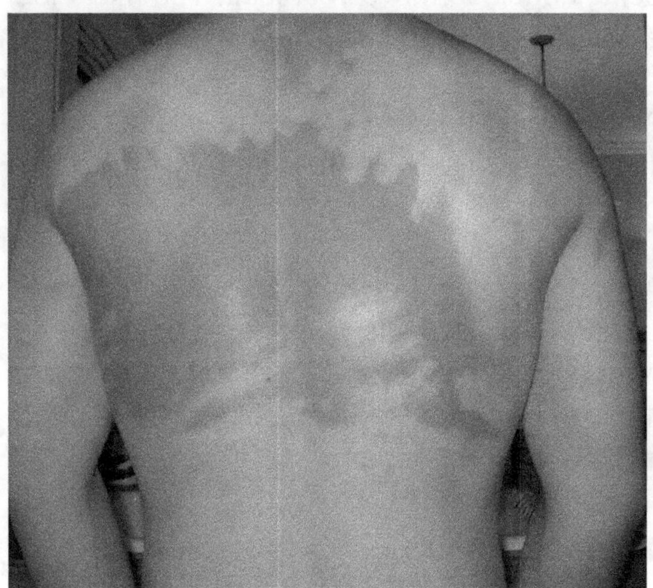

Method part 5

How to a Sprain or Strain

A sprain is a stretched or torn ligament. Ligaments are tissues that connect bones at a joint. Falling, twisting, or getting hit can all cause a sprain. Ankle and wrist sprains are common. Symptoms include pain, swelling, bruising, and being unable to move your joint. You might feel a pop or tear when the injury happens.

A strain is a stretched or torn muscle or tendon. Tendons are tissues that connect muscle to bone.

At first, treatment of both sprains and strains usually involves resting the injured area, icing it, wearing a bandage or device that compresses the area, and medicines. Later treatment might include exercise and physical therapy.

1. Control Swelling With RICE Therapy

RICE stands for:

- Rest the sprained or strained area. If necessary, use a sling for an arm injury or crutches for a leg or foot injury. Splint an injured finger or toe by taping it to an adjacent finger or toe.

- Ice for 20 minutes every hour. Never put ice directly against the skin or it may damage the skin. Use a thin towel for protection.

- Compress by wrapping an elastic (Ace) bandage or sleeve lightly (not tightly) around the joint or limb. Specialized braces, such as for the ankle, can work better than an elastic bandage for removing the swelling.

- Elevate the area above heart level if possible.

2. Manage Pain and Inflammation

- Give an over-the-counter NSAID (non-steroidal anti-inflammatory drug) like ibuprofen (Advil, Motrin), acetaminophen (Tylenol), or aspirin.

Knowing how to aid an injury as slight as a sprain or as severe as a broken bone can be the total difference in your survival and those who survive with you. Make preparations to have the needed first aid supplies that will come in handy when the zombies start to roam the earth.

THIS ONE IS FOR THE ALL LADIES

We know that the zombie apocalypse is not going to be a walk in the park for anyone. Least of all the women folk. Being a man is hard enough with all the responsibilities that will lay ahead. Women will have an even harder time adjusting to the conditions that a zombie fest will bring.

Apocalypse for the Ladies

There subject matter that is a bit sensitive to talk about however, I would be remise if I didn't broach the subject matter.

This is for the ladies. Women are the backbone of relationships for the most part. It is normally women that hold the family together. With that in mind, they are also different. They are not men. They usually cannot lift the weight a man can lift or carry as much as a man could under normal circumstances and emotionally they will break down and be a nervous wreck during the initial outbreak of zombie attacks. So there are few simple guidelines for women in the coming doom of the dead.

Let's face it, ladies, when the worst comes to the worst, you are probably going to have a harder time adapting to your new situation than men will. Not because women are weaker or smaller or can't function without high heels or whatever, but because your bodies are generally more high maintenance than men's' are. I don't mean more high maintenance in the sense women take longer to get dressed in the morning, but once society has broken down it's going to be a lot harder to find things that you're used to having, or alternatively, getting used to things that you are not used to having.

Body Hair

Yes, I know women usually portray themselves as graceful magic nymphs, all soft skin, and smooth legs, but once the SHTF, your leg hair isn't going to go anywhere in a hurry. While men will be relishing in the chance to finally grow a big ol' manly face beard, the majority of woman are not looking forward to growing their very own armpit beards.

So, ladies, what are your options? Well, if you've got enough money I'd recommend Laser Hair removal as a precaution. It probably won't stop hair growth forever, but after a regime, it reduces the total amount of hair in the treated area permanently. Intense pulsed light (IPL) is another option. It's cheaper and faster, but potentially not as effective.

If you have an epilator, it could work for a while. These pull hair out by the roots (ouch) and help prevent regrowth. However, they are powered by electricity and while you can get battery operated ones, I'd much rather put my batteries in a torch than in an epilator.

A pair of scissors can be used to trim away the worst of the hair (e.g. underarms) and have you looking generally well groomed for the post-apocalyptic world.

In the end, though, I think we'll have to eventually come to terms with our newfound hairiness. I mean, if men can grow forests on their legs, then why shouldn't we? It's not like anyone is going to see our legs under our thermals anyway.

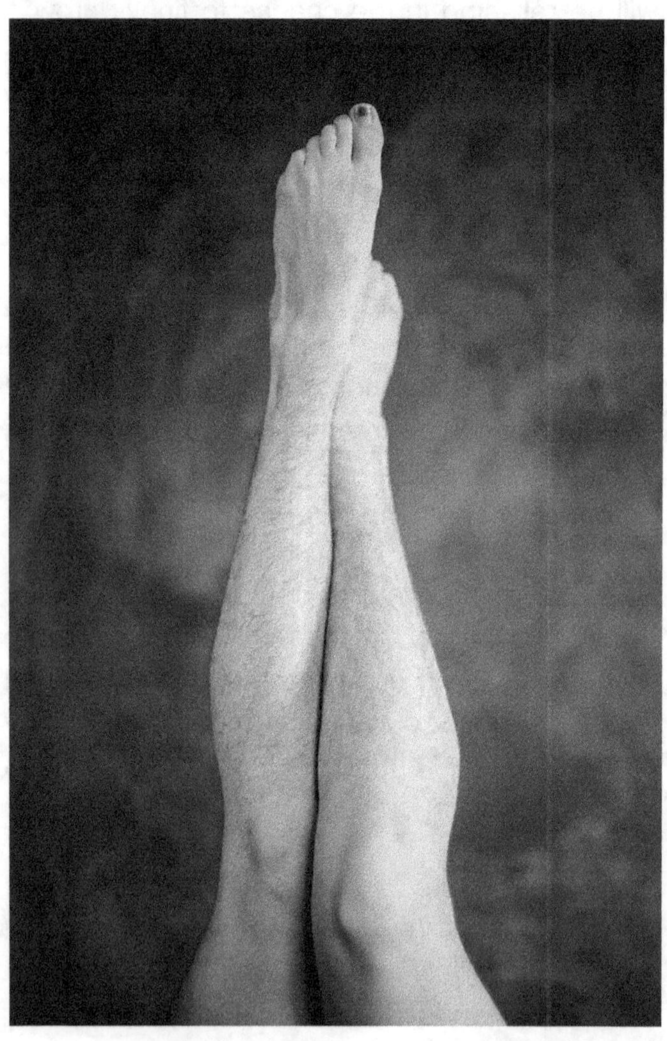

Head Hair

Ah, their crowning glory. A well-groomed head of hair is often what makes us feel human in the mornings. I sure as hell feel a lot more attractive when my hair is in place. Now think of all the things we have for our hair: shampoo, conditioner, dryers, straighteners, curlers and enough hair product to choke a colony of sea lions. I know this might not seem like a big deal to guys who can get out of the shower and shake their hair dry in 1 minute flat but long hair is quite high maintenance.

There is a very simple solution to this, however: chopping it off. I for one am going to hack my hair down as short as possible. Now ladies, I know it might be hard to cut your gorgeous locks off in the event of an apocalypse, but there are quite a few reasons why you should.

1)   Tangles. Unless you have a hairbrush with you, your hair is going to snarl up pretty quickly. Tying it back won't help- I've seen girls with ponytails they haven't brushed in a week and they basically have a knotted mat hanging down their back. Plaiting and finger combing might get you through for a while but eventually, your head will be a mess.

2)   Dirt. Yep, seeing as you won't be washing your hair anymore it's going to get dirty pretty quick. How often do you wash your hair normally? Once every two days? Every single day? You know how horrible your hair feels when you skip a day of washing- all that grease and grime- and that's basically how your hair is going to feel forever if you keep it long. It will also turn into a health hazard. You could be carrying around anything from radioactive ash to the cholera virus in your tangled, greasy hair.

3)   Bugs. If anything is going to survive the apocalypse it will be the nit because sometimes, the world just likes to make us miserable. However, nits won't be the only thing taking up residence on your scalp. A nice warm nest of long hair will be the perfect home for insects looking for somewhere to survive, and that's going to itch like a bitch.

All in all, shorter hair is better hair. It's cleaner, easier to look after, and you probably won't get sticks and stuff caught in it.

Teeth Care

This might be a section the guys will want to read too. Your teeth are so useful, and you'll definitely need a good set of gnashers to survive for any length of time. Now, stockpiles of toothpaste, toothbrushes, and floss only last for so long and eventually you're going to have to use more basic methods to keep your teeth in good working order.

Swilling your saliva around your mouth and licking your teeth often can be a good way to keep tartar build-up at a minimum, but you're really going to need something a bit scratchier to truly help your teeth. Early ways of ensuring good teeth included powdered pumice stone and scrubbing with sticks. The plant sap will replace toothpaste.

It's important to remember to clean between your teeth after meals to reduce bacteria. Get a sharp stick and a scrap of a mirror or something and spend a few minutes picking the food out of your teeth and you'll be a happier person for it. A toothache isn't fun at the best of times so getting it when you're traveling across a post-apocalyptic wasteland with your crew (or your faithful dog) is the last thing you want.

However, girls and boys, to ensure good dental health in the future you have to have good dental health now. If you can afford it, go to the dentist once a year. I don't care if you're scared of the dentist, do it.

A professional clean and check-up is the best thing for your teeth. And honestly, your dentist is not that scary. They're mostly nice chaps who are just tired of you screeching whenever they pull out a tool. If you can't afford to go to the dentist, and I realize that some of you would be, take very, very good care of your teeth. Dental floss, mouthwash, toothbrushes, the whole shebang. Always use a soft toothbrush as harder ones can damage your gums. Brush your teeth for at least five minutes twice a day, swill regularly with mouthwash and use dental floss religiously and you should be golden.

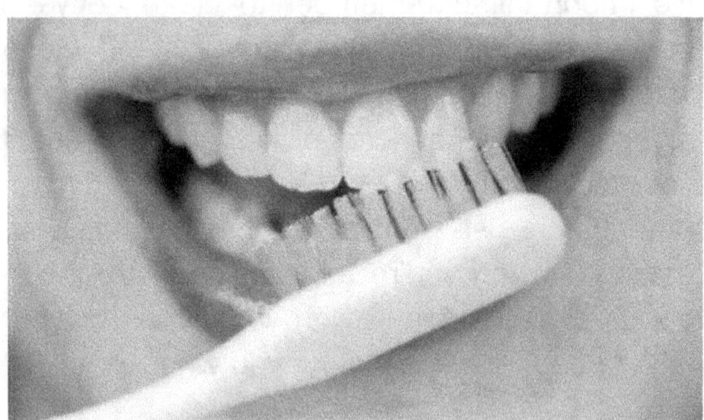

Knockers

I think it's important to dedicate a section of this article to your boobs, because let's face it, they're going to be a whole lot of trouble post-apocalypse. Once you get past how sexy they are (aww yeah) they're basically just jiggly bags that are going to make your lives harder, from accuracy with weapons to having CPR administered to running.

Honestly, the best advice I can offer is to stock up on some really good quality sports bras, the kind that basically straps your boobs down, while remaining relatively comfortable. They exist, you might have to fork out a bit of cash for them but they are so worth it, in your everyday life as well as for your emergency stockpile.

Depending on how big your ta-tas are, you might have problems with maneuvering. Your ability to fit through tight spaces, climb things and even lie on your stomach for long periods of time will be reduced the bigger your boobs are. Now, I know there isn't much you can do about this, except get a breast reduction If you're a serious survivalist but it is important to know your body's limits and not, say, get stuck and starve to death because you couldn't squash your upper body through a gap.

There's not a lot more I can offer in terms of boob- management, apart from the legend of the Amazonian women. It's said they used to lop off their right breast in order to increase their accuracy in archery, but I'm sure you won't have to go that far.

"Monthlies"

Your moon time. The red tide. Yes, your period. I'm sorry. I know this subject freaks a lot of people out and I'm going to try and keep it as brief as possible. The fact is, pads and tampons just aren't going to be readily available once society breaks down and you're going to have to find an alternative unless the idea of a red river flowing down your legs appeals to you. Well, look no further, for I am your guide!

If you're a regular pad user and can't abide the thought of sticking anything in you, menstrual sponges or cotton pads are available. These can be washed and re-used but you really should boil them before you use them again to get rid of bacteria. This can be problematic if water is at a premium.

Another option is the menstrual cup. This is emptied several times a day and should also be washed, but is smaller and will need less water to be cleaned effectively. These are a good option as they last for years and are non-toxic.

Now, you might think that with the breakdown of society the regulation of your menstrual flow won't be important. I mean, women in some African tribes just let it run, and what's so bad about that? Nothing, inherently, but you have to remember that post-apocalypse women are going to be living in a very different world and it will be so important to keep yourself as clean as possible. You wouldn't walk around with dried blood down one arm because it would attract bacteria, flies and other nasties. This is the same principle. Also, you will always want to keep your clothes as functionally clean as possible and, let's face it, layers of blood on the inside of your trousers is not good.

You have acquired a sweet stash of guns and ammo, your BOB is packed with necessary essentials and ready to make a quick retreat, and you brush up on your hunting/gathering skills at least once a month. Your food pantry is looking quite nice if you do say so yourself. But what if your home succumbs to a fire? Or you are on an overnight trip and are raided by thieves?

Fires can spring up suddenly from anything ranging from a faulty wiring or a lightning storm. As in the case of the recent wildfires in Colorado and California, some residents were only given minutes to evacuate. As part of your survival preparations, you need to consider such scenarios.

Never keep all your eggs in one basket. Separate the locations of your preps. Stash some in a travel trailer ready to hook up to your Bug Out Vehicle. Store a quantity in your food pantry/root cellar. And if you have family or trusted friends reasonably near you might be able to talk them into allowing you to store some stuff at their house. If your survival supplies are staggered in several different locations, not a fire, burglary, or another catastrophe will wipe you out in one fell swoop.

If you have the means, consider installing a sprinkler system, or reinforcing and fireproofing a root cellar that is not attached to your home.

Burying some supplies in waterproof containers is another great idea. Ideally digging into a hill above the water table, then waterproofing items with marine plastic wrapping to keep moisture out, and securing the entryway with a stone or metal doorway. Your supplies will be protected from a fire, flood or tornado, and you will have shelter if the dugout is large enough. The downfalls would be it would be a bit more difficult to bug out in a hurry, and not as well protected from burglary-especially if your dugout is a ways from your house.

As with anything, considering the options and having several plans is the greatest skill for survival.

Women Live Longer

In a recent study clinical physicians made an amazing discovery. Women normally outlive men in turmoil situations or hardship times. The study concluded that women will be more likely to survive than their male counterparts, according to this new research data.

Scientists over at the University of Southern Denmark analyzed times of feast or famine in the past 300 years including the Swedish famine of 1772-1773, life expectancy of enslaved people in Trinidad in 1813, the 1845 Irish potato famine, the measles epidemic in Iceland in 1842 and 1882, as well as the 1933 Ukraine famine. There was always one truth that remained consistent in their findings, on average: women lived longer than men. And this is regardless of age as well.

To determine the result, the scientists gathered birth and death records from the tragic periods in time. This doesn't come as much of a surprise though, since on average women live longer than men. (In the U.S., women are expected to live up to 86.6 years of age while men are expected to make it to 84.3 years.)

Other than every women being a badass like Michonne Character in *The* Walking *Dead-*

esque apocalyptic world, there's another reason for them surviving and thriving.

Most of the female advantage was due to differences in mortality among infants: baby girls were able to survive harsh conditions better than baby boys.

Women are the life-expectancy champions: They can expect to live longer than men almost anywhere in the world today. This pervasive inequality has intrigued researchers for decades. The cumulative corpus of research supports the conclusion that the gap has biological underpinnings modulated by social and environmental conditions. Deeper understanding could benefit from bio demographic research.

Support for a biological root of the gender gap in survival stems from studies of groups in which men and women have more similar lifestyles than in the general population, such as among nonsmokers or within religious groups such as active Mormons or cloistered monks and nuns. Findings indicate that, even though men and women in these groups have more similar lifestyles and men are exposed to fewer risk factors than zmen in the general population, a gender gap in life expectancy still persists.

Excess male mortality is also found among newborns and infants, when behavioral differences are unlikely to play a crucial role and social factors may be neutral or favor male survival. An untapped source of information is the reverse situation, when both men and women experience high, perhaps extreme, levels of mortality risk. A finding that men and women have similar life expectancies under these conditions would challenge the notion that the survival advantage of women is fundamentally biologically determined in all environments. Therefore, the study here was the survival of both sexes in populations enduring mortality crises.

While women have lower mortality than men in modern populations, evidence for a female survival advantage under crisis conditions is sparse. A well-known story concerns the Donner Party, a group of settlers that lost twice as many men as women when stranded for 6 months in the wilderness in the extreme winter of the Sierra Nevada Mountains.

Most survivors of that fateful event only survived after acts of cannibalism, eating the dead for sustenance. While accounts like this are anecdotal, a variety of studies provide evidence that women appear to survive cardiovascular diseases, cancers, and disabilities longer than men. However, the generality of this notion needs to be treated with caution, since findings on sex differences in survival after myocardial infarction and stroke are mixed.

Thus women live more years than men and are able to do so even though they are in bad health for a substantial part of those extra years of life.

A female survival advantage has also been documented in more recent and less extreme famines. During the Dutch Hunger Winter, the famines of Madras and Bombay, five south Asian famines, the Bengal famine, and the famine in the Matlab region, the overall effect of the crisis was greater for men than for women, even in regions where women usually had higher mortality than men.

This clearly shows that in an eventual catastrophe like that of man eating dead, women will fair far better than men. That is something to think about when selecting group members to fill out your Zombie Outbreak Response Team.

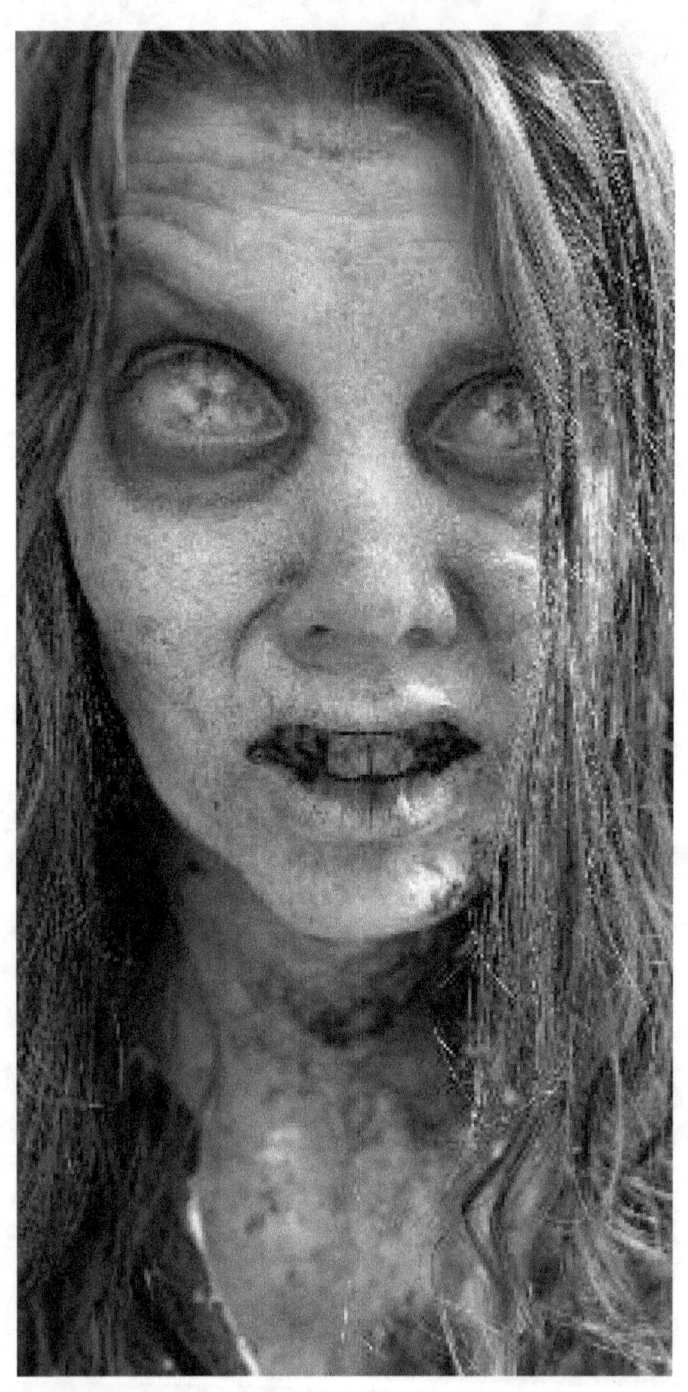

ARE YOU PREPARED?

Everyone knows it is coming, all signs point to the dead eventually rising and fighting back against the living and the inevitable all-out war that is sure to come of such an event, every day brings us all one step closer to this dark destiny.

THE BASIC SURVIVAL GUIDE FOR THE ZOMBIE APOCALYPSE

When the zombie apocalypse strikes, where will you be? Will you be one of the unlucky masses left behind as you scramble for all the things you need to survive a zombie apocalypse? Or will you be more prepared?

If you have read this guide cover to cover, chances are good you will have a pretty firm grasp of how to survive a zombie apocalypse, and you will be well ahead of the others when it comes to defending your property and braving the elements.

Of course, even the most diehard of fans is sure to be missing a few key items in their secret stash of goods, so as always, it is important to stay on top of things and prepare yourself for the future. Even those who are not fans of this popular show need to arm themselves now in order to be ready when the big day finally comes.

There is a lot to do to get ready for a zombie apocalypse, but if you work hard and collect plenty of zombie survival items, you too will be able to face your fate with courage. It is time to check out your list of Things to Survive a Zombie Apocalypse, and get your bunker ready for the battle.

Here are the top ten necessities to have prepared before the zombies hordes arrive.

1. Gather sufficient supplies to survive for 90 days.

Surviving after a major apocalyptic event is not going to be short-term since the entire country or the world is likely to be falling apart—there are no two ways around that reality. However, hopefully having three months of supplies will get you settled and going with your new self-sufficient habits. The more time you have dedicated to forming a plan when disaster does strike, the better. When preparing the supplies, think in two categories: basic survival and getting by, as outlined in the following two steps.

2.   Obtain and stockpile basic survival (the most important) items. Consider storing the following:

- Jugs of water

- Canned goods

- Vacuum-sealed goods

- Blanket and pillow

- Medications

- A weapon that you actually know how to use properly

- A knife (in addition to a weapon)

- Warm, long-sleeved clothing (if your climate requires it)

- Carrying bag (for moving and/or fleeing).

3.   Store supplies for just getting by. Think about having these items at your disposal:

- Batteries

- Flashlights

- Matches

- Pot (for cooking or boiling water)

- Plastic eating-ware (plate, mug, spoon, fork)

- Rope or twine

- Map

- Permanent markers (something to write with)

- Change of clothes

- Can opener

- Lighters

- Camp stove and propane

- Hatchet or ax

THE BASIC SURVIVAL GUIDE FOR THE ZOMBIE APOCALYPSE

- First aid book

- Sunglasses

- Duct tape

- Glow sticks

- Boots

- Extra pants

- Smartphone

- Water filters

- Other comfort items.

4. Prepare an emergency kit. Whether you're on the lookout from cannibals, flesh-eating super-bacteria, zombies, or a meteor, you'll need to think about your health. Here's a list for what you need to put in your emergency kit:

- Adhesive bandages, such as Band-Aids

- Gauze

- Medical tape

- Antibiotics (not for the zombie virus but for normal bacteria)

- Antiviral drugs (not for the zombie virus but for normal viruses)

- Ibuprofen (non-steroidal anti-inflammatory drug (NSAID))

- Acetaminophen/paracetamol (over-the-counter pain relief)

- Antihistamine

- Aspirin (over-the-counter pain relief)

- Laxative

- Iodine

THE BASIC SURVIVAL GUIDE FOR THE ZOMBIE APOCALYPSE

- Potassium Iodine

- Hand sanitizing liquid

- Candles

- A multi-use tool (aka a "hobo tool")

- Phone charger (preferably solar)

- Wood for burning

- Towels

- Life jackets, if your area is prone to flooding

- Extra warm clothes

- Paper towels

- Solar charger (see below)

- Pet food (enough for 30-90 days)

- Tweezers

- Plasters

- Safety pins

- Thermometer

- Superglue

- Toothpicks/needles.

FIRST AID KIT CHECKLIST

The first aid kit is your real lifeline. In any emergency. Even minor wounds like scrapes, scratches and cuts can infect and cause major problems. Some infections can lead to sepsis and lead to death. So with that in mind, keeping simple tools and medical supplies nearby is simpler than cutting off that leg.

- ☐ Bandages
- ☐ Hand Sanitizer
- ☐ Gauze Pads
- ☐ Gauze Roll(s)
- ☐ Scissors
- ☐ First Aid Tape
- ☐ Alcohol Swabs
- ☐ Cold Packs
- ☐ Thermometer
- ☐ Antibiotic Ointment
- ☐ Cortizone-10
- ☐ Ibuprophen
- ☐ Tylenol
- ☐ Antihistamine
- ☐ Bug Spray
- ☐ Sunscreen
- ☐ After Sun Lotion
- ☐ Alcohol
- ☐ Peroxide
- ☐ Cotton Swabs
- ☐ Flashlight
- ☐ Tweezers
- ☐ Nail Clippers

5. Keep yourself healthy against everything. You'll be dealing with everything from bouts to dysentery. Hospitals will cease existing and simple problems will seem a lot more daunting. If you or a family member has a specific ailment, stockpile medications for that, too.

6. Plan on how to prepare for the messier sides of the long-term. That's a nice way of saying, "Everybody poops." To keep hygiene from being an issue on top of everything else, pack the following:

- Toilet paper (a couple rolls will suffice)

- Menstrual products

- Toothbrush and toothpaste

- Plastic garbage bags and ties

- Shovel or trowel

- Bleach

- Soap and shampoo

7. Set up a communication system. Everyone in the household and close family and friends should have a communication system to communicate with family and friends. Communicate secret locations with your family members and friends using the radio.

• Keep batteries with your radio. The last thing you want is to presume you're prepared when you're really not. And if you have a loved one you're taking care of, make sure they have a radio and you're not keeping both of them for the two of you.

• When all else fails, work out how you will contact each other. This is when your permanent markers will come in handy. If the apocalypse strikes and you have left the house, write down where you are going, when you left, and if/when you'll be back on the wall, on a rock, on a nearby car, wherever you can find.

8. Use diesel-powered vehicles. Hoarding gasoline won't work; the chemicals that once kept it fresh will degrade it in time. After a year or so, it goes bad. Chances are gas stations will run out of gasoline but there could be some diesel left. In addition, all military diesel can run on other fuels as well, from rotten kerosene to fermented leaves. So invest in something that can handle the harder fuels.

• In the said vehicle, it's equally as likely that you'll be in it when all breaks loose, so pack a survival kit to keep in your car as well. Is there such a thing as being too prepared?

• If this isn't an option, make sure you have a bicycle laying around somewhere that's fully functioning. There will be a point when you need to cover large distances in a short amount of time.

9. Become a good shot. Knowing how to work a gun is going to keep you from either dying or being voted off the island.]. And while you're at it, buy a couple (if you haven't already).

• Regardless of who or what you'll be facing, this is probably a good idea. Anything menacing needs to be kept far, far away. Whatever or whomever your enemy, shooting them will probably increase your chances of not being attacked or eaten.

• Unless the apocalypse is due to some bacteria that are floating around in the air. In that case, get a gas mask. The people / zombies / menacing forces will probably still see you as an enemy.

10. Learn how to hunt.

• Master the art of the snare trap. If you're really scrappy with it, you need nothing but what nature provides you.

• If you're on the ocean or near a body of water, get to fishing or fly fishing. Your stock of baked beans and Spaghetti O's certainly isn't going to start spawning miraculously.

Key Professional Bump Key Set

You can never be too prepared for any situation, especially a zombie attack. Assuming you can't get your hands on an AK-47 or an antidote, you're going to need some supplies. You need to come up with a list of the MUST HAVE Zombie Attack survival gear.

Everyone knows that the best weapons, health packs and secret notes are behind locked doors. Everyone also knows that there's no way to kick down or cut through, even the flimsiest of locked doors. That's why you need a Professional Bump Keys to help you navigate your way through a zombie infested city on lockdown.

Weapons to Survive the Zombie Apocalypse

Amendment two of the U.S. Constitution guarantees the right of the people to keep and bear arms. But there is a wide range of opinions these days regarding personal possession of firearms. Regardless of your opinion, if there are individual's intent upon doing you harm, and the police are unable to help you, your chances of survival will improve if you are armed. Are you willing to risk the welfare of your family to the whims of a marauding gang, or will you take steps to protect the ones you love?

This is obviously not an area where overkill is desirable. You would not want to kill or severely injure someone unless it was absolutely necessary. So I believe that your first line of defense should be pepper spray or mace, or perhaps a Taser or stun gun. Everyone in your family should at least carry pepper spray during dangerous times. They should also practice using it. Pepper spray alone may be sufficient to drive off a lone individual who is not too intent upon having your possessions. After all, he will probably reason that there will be an easier target down the street, and he will probably be right. A Taser or stun gun will be an even better deterrent.

If you can avoid it you will not want to get close enough to an offender to use a stun gun or pepper spray. Be aware that pepper spray was originally made as a deterrent for wild animals. Animals rely on their keen sense of smell for the majority of their senses. The Spray was meant to be used outdoors, directly in to the snout or nose of an attacking or aggressive animal such as a bear or wild dog. Since its original inception it has been a staple for law enforcement and self-defense for women promotions. Although it does burn and irritate the human eyes and skin it is often defused easily with water and many people have been known to tough it out and continue to attack even after a heavy dose has been sprayed directly in their face. Another factor to consider is that the pepper spray was produced and designed to be sprayed outdoors. The use of it in a confined space indoors can be just as detrimental to the victim as much as the attacker. The noxious propellant once sprayed, fills the air, so anyone within the effected range (0 ft. - 15 ft.) will likely feel the sting and irritation of the chemical gas as well. This usually means the defender or person using he spray.

A BB gun or powerful air-soft gun that shoots plastic BB's might prove to be another handy deterrent. It could allow you to take care of problems from a greater distance than that required to use your stun gun or pepper spray, and again without doing too much harm. A BB will sting but it is not likely to pierce the skin.

Avoid shooting at the face or head, unless your intent is to do some damage. Perhaps someone is stealing fruit from your trees. If a verbal warning doesn't work, the sting of a BB on their leg or back might convince them that you are serious. If the BB doesn't work, most likely the sound of a shotgun fired into the air will do the job nicely.

Unless you are an experienced gun owner, I do not recommend that you purchase a firearm unless you also take a firearms or hunter's safety class. Check at any location where guns or hunting licenses are sold for information on the classes in your area. Everyone in your family who is old enough to hunt or use a firearm should also take the class. Then you should take your firearms to a practice range and become proficient with their use. Always keep your guns and ammunition locked up and out of the reach of children.

Your survival supplies should include, not only the weapons mentioned above, but plenty of ammunition as well. During a prolonged emergency, ammunition might also serve as a useful item for barter, so don't fail to stock up. When picking a weapon to survive the zombie apocalypse, one must consider what would be the BEST weapon over what would be a good weapon or even the COOLEST weapon. Many factors come into play when choosing a weapon. Storage space in your shelter, the weight and storage space available if you are on the move, how loud said weapon would be etc.

Firearms

1) Semi-automatic magazine-fed rifles

Though much debate could be done about the fine-grained specifics regarding individual models, there is no weapon more suitable to a wide variety of situations than an auto loading magazine-fed rifle. Able to be loaded and readied quickly, and capable of providing sustained, accurate fire from arm's length out to standoff ranges at a rate as rapidly as the shooter can comfortably acquire targets, this sort of weapon would prove useful in nearly all survival situations, ranging from hunting and taking small and large game to defending oneself against other humans, and everything in between. Depending on the cartridge chambered, the shooter may also be able to defeat armored targets and light barriers as well.

2) Semi-automatic magazine-fed handguns

Almost as important as a solid long gun is the sidearm that should accompany it. With operating characteristics similar to its larger cousins, a sidearm provides the shooter with an immediately accessible secondary offensive option or reliable defensive choice that maintains a safe distance from the target in the event that their primary firearm runs dry on ammunition, malfunctions, or otherwise fails. Such a weapon can be easily drawn and quickly reloaded, and ensures that barring some extraordinary circumstance, the shooter will always be armed.

3) Crossbows

Some manner of crossbow would likely be as valuable as any firearm, and would provide a survivor with a means of eliminating single targets with a degree of subtlety not afforded by other ranged weaponry. Aimed in a manner similar to a rifle, crossbows would prove much easier for most individuals to accustom themselves to, especially those who already possess experience in handling long guns. As an added benefit, any ammunition expended could be recovered and reused, provided that it was not damaged by the initial use.

4) Manually-operated shotguns

While not optimal choices compared to most other firearms, due to their relatively limited ammunition capacity, short range compared to rifles, and bulky ammunition, shotguns are an attractive choice provided there are no other alternatives. Though the method of reloading and operating most shotguns can be off-putting and difficult for most shooters (since each cartridge must be individually inserted into the weapon's magazine), their reliability and somewhat forgiving patterning of shot at moderate ranges may be serviceable enough to keep someone alive until a better weapon could be acquired. Also not to be overlooked is that most manually-operated shotguns can chamber and fire a wide variety of ammunition types provided that the appropriate size of ammunition is being used.

5) Revolvers

Though their limited capacity and the relatively complicated method of reloading inherent to most models has relegated revolvers to a practically novel status in most contexts, like shotguns, one would be a welcome addition to the arsenal of someone lacking better options, and - depending on the cartridge the weapon is originally chambered for - may allow for the usage of several different cartridge types.

THE BASIC SURVIVAL GUIDE FOR THE ZOMBIE APOCALYPSE

Various Weapons for the Apocalypse

THE BASIC SURVIVAL GUIDE FOR THE ZOMBIE APOCALYPSE

Various Weapons for the Apocalypse

Revolvers for Defense

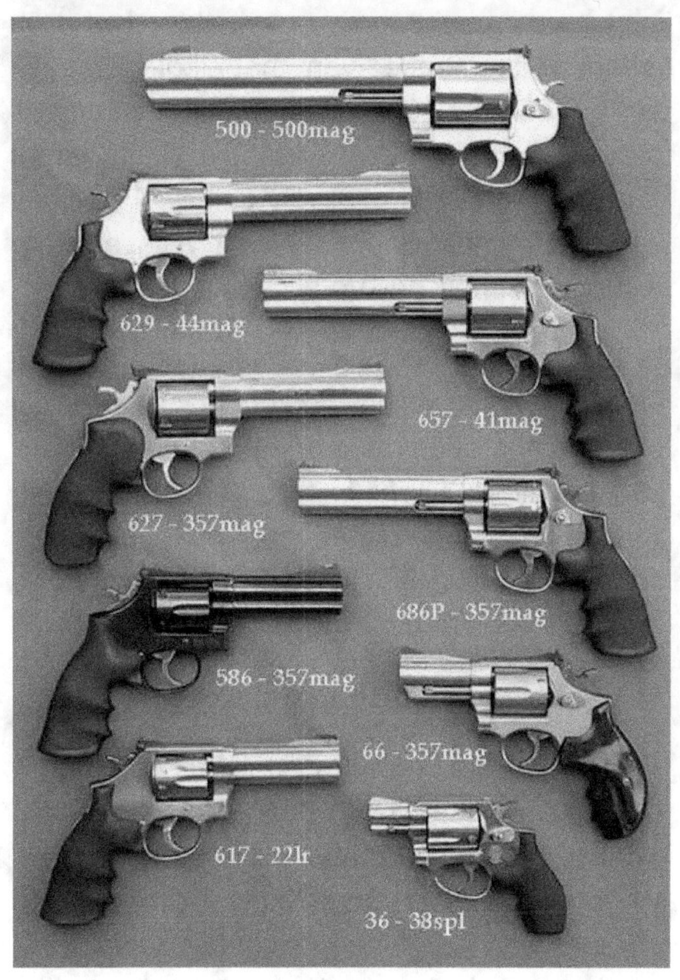

Melee Weapons

It can easily be seen that a decent melee implement could be a valuable last-ditch defensive tool in the event that all other means are out of reach, or if all ammunition has been expended, or in the case that a single target must be eliminated relatively quietly. They may also be the most viable choice in a case where a survivor simply has no access to firearms.

Unlike most ranged weapons, melee implements are reliant entirely on the physical strength and endurance of the wielder, and are only practically useful in emergencies, as even well-trained individuals in peak physical condition tire very quickly when delivering blows strong enough to destroy the human skull.

1) Machete or similar edged weapon

A machete, while offering nominal utility as a tool for clearing paths through thick vegetation, would offer much greater utility as a weapon. While not the most immediately deadly weapon on the face of things, a heavy, reinforced machete or similar one-handed, bladed melee weapon has the capability of not only killing provided the user can deliver a sharp blow to the head, but can easily disable humanoid attackers, which generally requires less

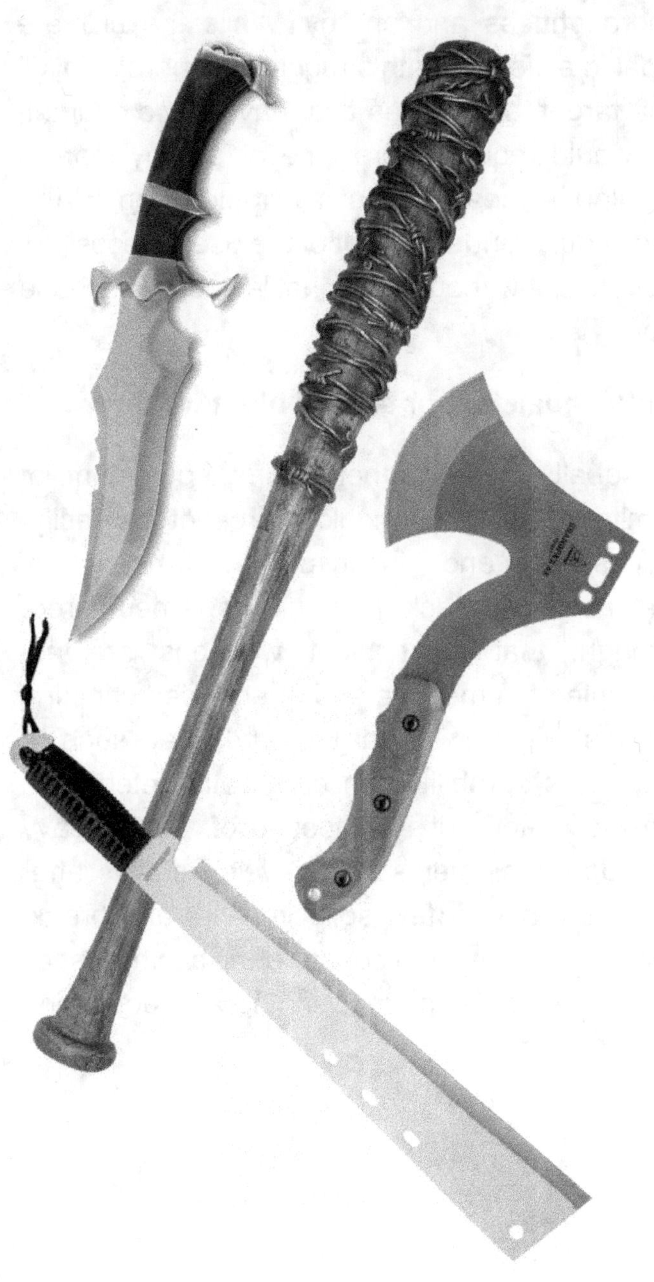

thoroughness and energy. While the ultimate goal in a life-or-death struggle is generally to kill the target, sometimes this may not be optimal, or would require more time or energy than is available, meaning that a simple chop to the legs could render pursuit of the user impossible, as a target without functional legs cannot chase you.

2) Baseball bat, or similar blunt weapon

Baseball bats or other sports equipment of similar construction could represent an easily-accessible and inconspicuous means of defense and attack. It should be remembered, though, that most blunt weapons are not capable of immediate and guaranteed crippling or disabling of a target, and that such a weapon's durability can be greatly determined by the material it's composed of. Even heavy wooden implements can develop cracks after only a relatively few solid impacts and break, while their aluminum counterparts can be just as vulnerable to damage, bending and deforming in short order.

3) Crowbar

Crowbars offer great utility to a survivor, enabling their user to force doors or destroy their facings, pry open containers, easily shatter most glass, and effect other means of surreptitious entry, but they also represent a decent last-ditch melee option. While not optimal, given their shape and construction, a crowbar could be used as a solid blunt weapon that can be relied upon not to break after a few swings.

There are many more choices for weapons, these are merely a few sections that could do the trick in such situations as needed.

When choosing a weapon it is important to remember that they are very personal and each person may feel more comfortable with one weapon over another for a myriad of different reasons. Ease of use, recoil, loading, cleaning, size, power, allowable ammunition and access are all varied and acceptable reason for selecting one weapon over another. None are wrong, but there are exceptions to that rule. The use of any weapon should be the accuracy of its use. Meaning that you would not use a shotgun for a distance precision shoot. You would normally use a long rifle with a sight and scope attachment to get the benefit of the weapon.

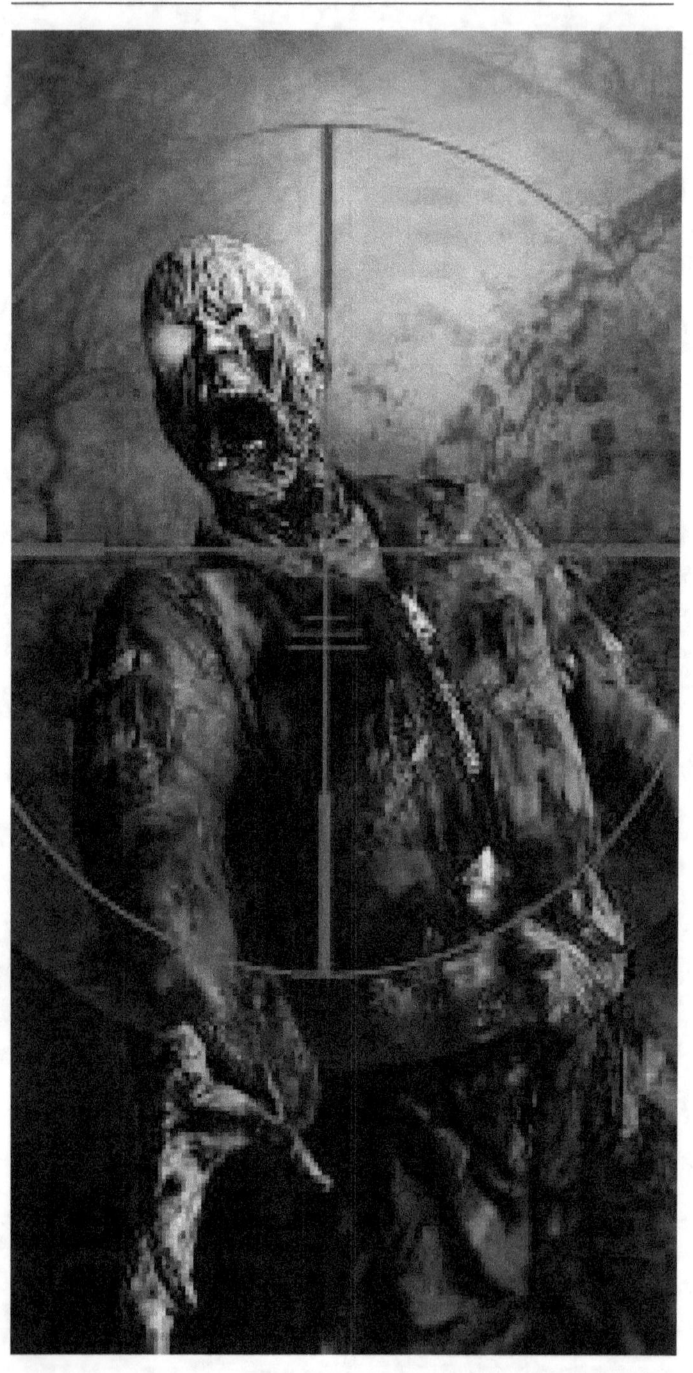

Therefore, using a long sword to cut a piece of rope where a small knife would do would also be the better choice given the situation.

Understanding that in warfare the range and tactical use of the weapon are important to the task at hand. If the zombie were within 10 feet of you during an attack, using a rifle to shoot a zombie is wieldy, where a small revolver or automatic handgun would suffice and be better suited to the task. Knowing the difference and balancing out the needs and necessities of weapon use for the defensive or offensive position.

Military or combative tactics play an essential role in the selection of weaponry. Learning the practical and advantageous use of the proper weapon can mean the difference in actual life skills and true survival during an incursion against a marauding band of looters set out to steal or an attacking horde of zombies out to feast on the living.

LIFE AT THE READY

What will happen if society collapses? What would you do if there's no one to help you or your family? Disaster preparedness is more than worrying—it's also about being practical, preparing for realistic scenarios and being ready for the unpredictable. An apocalypse is unlikely, but you'll need to know what to do in case it happens.

You're going to need all of your instincts to survive, but you can't be on red alert all the time. Instead, you should get used to condition yellow. That means being aware and ready to respond at any time. You used to refer to this state as sleeping with one eye open, but it's more than that. Observe everything around you.

Watch and learn. When are the zombies most active? Is it in your area, as has been reported or were the experts wrong? There is often misinformation flying around in a panic, so use your common sense. Your survival always depends on it.

Keep a notebook in your pocket and record all observations, and for the love of all things holy, share this information with other non-infected people you might encounter. Survival isn't a solo effort.

Gather an effective team. You're going to need to cover each other's backs so you can get the rest you need. Remember that these need to be people you can trust. If you have someone who freezes in fear or a panicky screamer, he or she is a liability, not an asset. Instead of helping you when you need it, you'll be saving them over and over again. Oftentimes those sorts of people will be your own children. There's little you can do about this. You have the survival of a species to look after, and, unlike in the movies, you don't get a rewrite if the ending isn't to your liking.

Important survival items

Often survival practitioners will carry with them a "survival kit". This consists of various items they deem necessary or useful for short durations in the wilderness. Supplies in a survival kit normally contain items like a sharp knife generally a Swiss army knife, matches, first aid box, fish hooks, sewing kit and a LED flashlight.

This is no three-hour tour. An effective team should include at least the following: a kick-butt ninja for stealth attacks and midnight supply runs; that kid you knew in high school who was always making his own ammo and blowing things up – he was weird then, now he's essential – one biomedical engineer to concoct experimental vaccines on the spot – bonus points if she's also a crack shot; and a mechanic who can take all those scraps of cars along the road and turn them into a steam-rolling tank.

Set up a meeting place for your family outside of town. Practice meeting there. Figure out seven unique routes to get there and three ways to contact one another if the cell service is out. Establish how long you will wait for each other before moving on to a safer location. Figure out how you would get back in touch if you were separated for long. You do not want to have to wait in the open on the chance that your family is going to show up. The more nimble you are, the greater your chances of survival.

Now that you know what to watch for, it's time to plan ahead and ensure your survival. Because once the zombies are among us, you'll know it. The right know-how plus a little luck can help you survive anything from a tornado to the zombie pandemic.

THE BASIC SURVIVAL GUIDE FOR THE ZOMBIE APOCALYPSE

Preparing for an Emergency

The best thing you can do for yourself right now before the outbreak happens, it is a matter of "when," not "if," is to gather together that emergency kit you've always meant to pull together. Think about what life would be like if you were trapped in your house for a week or two. What if you had no electricity or had to escape on foot to the wilderness? What if you needed to make a shelter? You have the luxury of time right now, don't waste it. Pull these items together:

• Food – At least one week's worth. At least. Two months would be better.

• Water – One gallon per person per day.

• Flashlight and batteries.

• Survival tools – Matches, a knife, scissors, duct tape, and more.

• Emergency radio – Preferably hand-cranked rather than battery operated.

• Two-way radios.

• Weather-appropriate clothing – This includes good walking shoes and warm clothing.

•	Outdoor supplies – At least a tent and sleeping bag. Plastic sheeting or a tarp can be used as shelter or to collect water.

•	Personal hygiene items and medication.

•	First aid kit – Bandages, disinfectant, and gloves.

•	Important personal papers.

•	Cash and other valuables – This does not mean your XBox unless you are planning on using it as a hammer.

•	Extra gasoline.

•	Maps.

•	Don't forget to pack specific things your kids and pets need.

You may never use these items, at least we hope you don't need to (especially for a zombie apocalypse). For a more complete list, visit FEMA's website.

Food

Culinary root tubers, fruit, edible mushrooms, edible nuts, edible beans, edible cereals or edible leaves, edible moss, edible cacti, and algae can be searched and if needed, prepared (mostly by boiling). With the exception of leaves, these foods are relatively high in calories, providing some energy to the body. Plants are some of the easiest food sources to find in the jungle, forest or desert because they're stationary and can thus be had without exerting much effort. Skills, and equipment (such as bows, snares, and nets) necessary to gather animal food in the wild include animal trapping, hunting, and fishing. Focusing on survival until rescued by presumed searchers, the Boy Scouts of America especially discourages foraging for wild foods on the grounds that the knowledge and skills needed are unlikely to be possessed by those finding themselves in a wilderness survival situation, making the risks (including the use of energy) outweigh the benefits.

Navigation

These two pictures of the same tree trunk in the Northern Hemisphere are an example of a navigational terrain feature. The left picture shows the northern side of a trunk, where darker and more humid microclimatic conditions favor moss growth. The right picture is south, with sunnier and drier conditions, less favorable for moss growth. The shady side is not always opposite the noon side.

Survival situations can often be resolved by finding a way to safety, or a more suitable location to wait for rescue. Types of navigation include:

•   Celestial navigation, using the sun and the night sky to locate the cardinal directions and to maintain the course of travel

•   Using a map, compass or GPS receiver

•   Dead reckoning

•   Natural navigation: navigating using the condition of surrounding objects (i.e. moss on a tree, snow on a hill)

Mental preparedness

The mind and its processes are critical to survival. The will to live in a life and death situation often separates those that live and those that do not. Stories of heroic feats of survival by regular people with little or no training but a strong will to live are not uncommon.

To the extent that stress results from testing human limits, the benefits of learning to function under stress and determining those limits may outweigh the downside of stress. There are certain strategies and mental tools that can help people cope better in a survival situation, including focusing on manageable tasks, having a Plan B available and recognizing denial.

Remember that the idea of prepping for a disaster is to prepare yourself for the worst. Training and retraining yourself of specific skill sets that will allow you to better survive in case of a disaster or an overwhelming herd of undead. Practice by going camping to hone your newly acquired knowledge of survival. Prep your house and your family so that they will be ready in case of such emergencies. Learning as a family can bring you together and keep you safe during any disaster.

Survival manuals

A survival manual is a book used as a reference in situations where a human's survival is threatened - expected or unexpected. Typically it will cover both preparation and guidance for dealing with eventualities.

There are many different types of survival manuals, but most have a section of standard advice. These are sometimes republished for public distribution: for example the SAS Survival Handbook, United States Army Survival Manual (FM 3-05.70) and the United States Air Force Survival Manual (AF 64-4).

The Basic Survival guide for the Zombie Apocalypse is the best book I can recommend and if you are reading this book now then you are a big step ahead in your prep for the coming disaster.

Even if the zombies don't come then you have a great way to prep for any other disaster such as hurricanes, tornados, Earthquakes, floods or any other sort of foul weather or common disaster that may befall you. Keeping a book like this handy will be a ready-made handbook filled with information to keep you alive in case such an emergency arises.

How to deal with a zombie.

• It important to aim for the skull when shooting a zombie to take out the cerebral cortex (believed to be infected with an unknown pathogen, possibly containing a genetically modified rabies virus crossed with a bio-engineered virus that mimics "the munchies" and likely conceived in an underground lab at Bethesda, Maryland). If you hit any other area, you will only make them meaner and more determined than ever to cannibalize you (and one bite will infect you, so you better hope they finish you off at that point).

• If you have a machete or other sharp object, you must cut off their head to incapacitate them. Unless you have a machete you can quickly use to decapitate the zombie (say you only have a sharp knife) it is recommended you sneak up behind them, jump on their back, and hack away at their neck until you are able to separate the head from the body. (Do not allow the head to bite you; it will remain animated and that rabid mouth will infect you if biting into you.)

• My opinion is to not get too much of a large group, always have a fat person as an extra life as fat people will be first picked off.

* wear a fake zombie suit and pretend to be a zombie

* Apply for a position with Umbrella Corporation (showcased in Resident Evil and movie sequels) so that you will get their anti-zombie virus vaccine (an employee benefit). Make sure your resume doesn't include any hint that you have a conscience, empathy, or other qualities Umbrella recruiters will screen out.

* Distasteful as it may seem, the best method of distracting zombies is to push an obese member of your group into a group of attacking zombies, then run like hell.

* Upon learning of a zombie infestation you NEED: A fast vehicle, fill it with fuel. The best choice is a mobile home or a van (NO CONVERTIBLES!) bring all the water you can.

* A Shotgun and all the shells you can fit into your vehicle.

* The best place to hide from zombies is a hot air balloon or an airplane (assuming there are no zombies on the plane). In a hot air balloon you won't need to refuel, and you will be able to see where the zombies congregate and stay away from them.

You won't need to hide as long as the zombies don't sprout wings. All science notes that as far as any evidence suggest, zombies cannot fly. So you will be relatively safe. Helicopters, planes, air balloons and anything else aerial you'll be pretty safe from the zombie infestation below.

•   Try to find a temporary refuge to get to the safe zone.

•   A crossbow is better than a gun because it may get multiple zombies and is silent. A chainsaw is equally as good, but loud. You need to have at least a baseball bat or fire ax.

•   Lasers are the best defense because they turn zombies to dust.

•   Never wear heels, or dress shoes unless you are a British secret agent. You are most likely to twist your ankle when zombies are around, for unknown reasons.

Protection "GET" Check List:

1. [ ] Pepper spray or Mace for each adult family member
2. [ ] Taser or stun gun
3. [ ] Intruder alarms
4. [ ] Firearms
5. [ ] Extra ammunition
6. [ ] Etc.

Protection "DO" Check List:

1. [ ] Install deadbolt locks on all outside doors
2. [ ] Make sure house is secure at all points of possible entry
3. [ ] Install intruder alarms
4. [ ] Enroll each adult family member in a firearms safety class
5. [ ] Practice using peppers spray or Mace. (Don't practice on a real person!)
6. [ ] Visit local firearms practice range and become proficient with the use of our firearms
7. [ ] Sign up for a martial arts class.
8. [ ] Etc.

Common myths

Some survival books promote the "Universal Edibility Test". Allegedly, it is possible to distinguish edible foods from toxic ones through a series of progressive exposures to skin and mouth prior to ingestion, with waiting periods and checks for symptoms. However, many experts including Ray Mears and John Kallas rejected this method, stating that even a small amount of some "potential foods" can cause physical discomfort, illness, or death.

Many mainstream survival experts have perpetuated the act of drinking urine in times of dehydration, however, the United States Air Force Survival Manual (AF 64-4) instructs that this technique should never be applied. Several reasons include the high salt content of urine, potential contaminants, and sometimes bacteria growth, even though popular belief is that urine is "sterile".

Natural disasters come in all shapes and sizes. Hurricanes, earthquakes, flooding and landslides, forest fires, tornadoes, and many other disasters can present themselves unexpectedly. They all can have a major disruptive effect on our lives.

Being prepared for these events can help you and your family ride out the storm and come out on the other end safely and better able to handle post-disaster situations.

Here are 10 tips to help you become more prepared for natural disasters?

1. For the possibility of flooding, have an ax and life preservers available.

Stash an ax and life preservers in the upper story, or attic, of your home. Remember, most of the drowning victims of Hurricane Katrina were people who stayed in their homes and found themselves trapped by rising waters with no place to go. Many drowned in their attics, unable to break through the roof to the outside. A few bucks spent on these items ahead of time could save your life!

2. Water is critical.

Water is absolutely essential for human survival; it plays a part in all of the body's biochemical reactions. You may not believe it, but most of us could survive for several weeks without food, yet a single day without water in extreme heat can kill a person. Water requirements vary depending on activity level and temperature. The absolute minimum for survival, with little or no activity and cool conditions, is about one quart of drinking water per day, and two quarts of water per day will usually sustain moderate activity at an acceptable level of comfort under moderate conditions (you will feel somewhat dehydrated). More than 1 quart of water every hour can be required to perform heavy physical labor under extremely hot conditions. Typically allow for at least one gallon per person per day.

Clean drinking water can easily become unavailable before, during, and after a natural disaster due to supply shortages, contamination, and power outages. Store water today to meet your needs in an emergency.

3.   Fill your bathtub and tap off your toilets.

After a major disaster hits, the public water system may be polluted or entirely shut down for weeks. Immediately fill your bathtubs, sinks, and other available containers with water. This will provide your household with a short-term supply of clean, potable water.

There is also a supply of clean, potable water in the toilet tanks, hot-water heater, and piping in your house. When you notice that the tap water has stopped flowing, conserve the water in your toilet tanks (the tanks, not the bowl, contain potable water) and immediately notify all other occupants to not flush the toilets. (CAUTION: Do not drink the toilet tank water if you use an automatic toilet cleaner with blue toilet water).

4. Drain your water heater and pipes.

Water heaters are supplied with a vent located near the top of the tank and a drain near the bottom of the tank. Open the top vent (pull on the little lever on the spigot) and drain the tank into containers as needed. If there are dirt and sediment in the water coming out of the tank, do not discard this water. Simply allow the sediment to settle and drink the water off the top. Make sure you turn off the electricity or gas to your water heater before draining or it will be ruined! Crack an upper faucet and open a lower hose bib or faucet to drain a few gallons of water out of your home's piping.

5. Use water filters and treatment chemicals.

I know from experience that most anyone will drink from the worst, scummiest water after having gone without water for more than a day in extreme heat! If you must evacuate your home, carrying a personal water supply on your back would be extremely difficult (at a gallon per person per day, a family of four would consume 100 lbs of water in three days). Flood waters are usually extremely contaminated with farm waste, human sewage, and industrial chemicals, so I highly recommend that you purchase a bacteriological back-country-type water filter that has a carbon core to also remove toxic chemicals, bad tastes, and odors. You can chemically treat surface water with household tincture of iodine (5 drops per quart) and pure chlorine bleach (4 drops per quart) and allowing water to stand for 30 minutes. See Chapter 5 of When Technology Fails for full water treatment details and my personal water filter recommendations. (I design these things for a living, so I know what I am talking about). Boiling for just one minute will kill all water-borne organisms, but will do nothing to remove toxic chemicals, bad tastes, and odors.

6. Put together a 72-Hour Grab-and-Run Kit.

Every family should have at least one Grab-and-Run kit that can be thrown in the car on a moment's notice, or carried on your back if the need should arise. Grab-and-Run kits should provide the basic emergency food, water, shelter, and first aid supplies that you and your family will need to survive the critical first three days after a disaster. See my other WSID article: 72-Hour "Grab-and-Run" Survival Kits.

7. Store your Grab-and-Run Kits in "dry packs."

If you live in hurricane country or other areas with potential for serious storms and flooding, I strongly recommend that you purchase a "dry pack" for each of your grab-and-run kits. A "dry pack" is a special combination backpack and waterproof bag used by river guides. They have removable padded shoulder straps, are made of extremely tough, waterproof material, and are 100% sealed against water intrusion. So in addition to keeping your stuff dry in a deluge, they will also double as floatation devices to help keep you afloat in flood waters. A "dry pack" stocked and ready to go for every member of your family is cheap insurance!

8. Keep a colloidal silver generator.

After a natural disaster, homemade colloidal silver will purify drinking water and will help fight infection and viruses when high-tech pharmaceuticals may be unavailable or ineffective. All hospitals use silver-based ointments to fight infection in severe burn victims, where traditional antibiotics are simply not enough to fight the infection over large areas of burned skin.

9. Formulate a disaster plan,

Including out of town contacts (relatives, family friends, etc.) and a central meeting place where your family should meet if separated and local communications are cut. When a widespread disaster strikes, you will usually be able to reach friends or family outside of the disaster area long before local communications can be re-established. See the Preparedness Checklist on page 50 of When Technology Fails for full details.

10. Use waterproof LED headlamps.

I highly recommend that you purchase a waterproof back-country-type headlamp with LED bulbs. Headlamps leave your hands free to carry or work on things. LED bulbs to use a fraction of the power, are far more shock resistant and last far longer than traditional light bulbs, so your batteries (don't forget to stock spares) last many times longer.

Outdoor Survival Tips

Cities are your enemy in case of zombie attack. Suddenly your friendly corner grocer is anything but. Your best chance is to get away from civilization. Zombies will freeze in subzero temperatures, but so will you. Avoid the fate of many of the civilians in World War Z by preparing for a life out of doors if not in the Arctic. Ancient legends hold that zombies once attacked an Inuit village. Not one zombie survived.

• Slow moving water is less likely to carry bacteria, so drink from the edge of a stream.

• You can follow a stream to a river to a lake or ocean.

• Remember that your fire is visible in the night and downwind zombies can smell it no matter what time of day it is.

• Maintaining body temperature is critical. Dress in layers and try not to let yourself sweat, because as the sweat evaporates you can get colder than you thought.

• You need to maintain circulation, especially in the cold, so make sure your clothes and boots aren't too tight.

•   Stay dry if at all possible. If not, get dry quickly, even if it means getting more naked in front of strangers than you'd like.

•   Buy a book now on what's edible in the forest and memorize it. You'll be glad later.

•   Learn to read the clouds. They'll tell you what kind of weather to expect in the next 24 hours.

First, you get that creepy-crawly feeling running down your spine. Crouched low in the shadows, you shift your ax from one hand to the other. You think you're alone, but your instincts are telling you otherwise. Then it happens — screaming out from darkness comes the biggest, baddest, ugliest walking dead you've ever seen. Should you attack? Should you run? Or should you call in reinforcements? These are good questions to ask when dealing with a zombie outbreak. And we have a list of tips that will keep you on your toes — and alive – during a zombie outbreak.

Science says zombies — lumbering, flesh-eating corpses — don't exist in the real world. Except in rare emergency room situations, dead people can't come back to life, and even if they could, there is little reason to suspect they'd wake up with a sudden, unquenchable appetite for human flesh.

Still, every time a criminal act of cannibalism makes headlines, the Internet comes alive with chatter about an impending zombie apocalypse. A spate of flesh-chomping that occurred earlier this year, including the famous "Miami zombie attack," even prompted the Centers for Disease Control and Prevention to reassure people that the zombie apocalypse isn't coming.

But judging by the ongoing interest in zombies, not everyone was convinced. For all those who fear that the living dead really could rise up and go on a mass cannibalistic rampage à la the classic 1968 film "Night of the Living Dead," we've put together a little guide to help you prepare for the worst.

Fortunately, these tips will help you weather many other types of disasters, too, from hurricanes to tornadoes to pandemic virus outbreaks. So whether or not you believe in the living dead, read on.

Emergency plan

When chaos ensues, you won't be able to think rationally. Your survival may depend on whether you came up with an emergency plan in advance. The plan should apply in cases of a flood, earthquake, and blackout or, of course, when a pack of zombies starts clambering across your front yard — and make sure everyone in your household has it down.

Here's what your emergency plan should entail, according to the CDC:

1.   Pick two meeting places for your family, one close to your home and another farther away. These come in handy if family members are separated when an emergency kicks in, or if an immediate evacuation from your home becomes necessary (such as in the case of a fire).

2.   Identify the types of emergencies that are possible in your area. Besides a zombie apocalypse, this may include floods, tornadoes, or earthquakes.

3.   Make a list of emergency contacts. This should include local officials like the police and fire department, as well as a more geographically-distant contact whom you can

call during an emergency. This person can notify the rest of your loved ones about your status.

4. Plan your evacuation route, both out of your home and out of your town. Make sure you know whose house you will go to in case of an emergency (zombie-related or otherwise) in your area.

Good luck out there. If zombies are real, you'll need it.

This equation could spell your doom: (bN)(S/N)Z = bSZ. That is if you ever found yourself in the midst of a zombie pandemic.

That's because the calculation describes the rate of zombie transmission, from one walking dead individual to many, according to its creators, Robert J. Smith?, a mathematics professor at the University of Ottawa who spells his name with a "?" at the end, and his students. Smith's work has inspired other researchers to create zombie mathematical models, which is published with Smith's work in the book, "Mathematical Modeling of Zombies" (University of Ottawa Press, 2014).

Though of course done tongue-in-cheek, Smith's study demonstrates why zombies are the viruses of the monster world. Their likeness to viruses makes the creatures ideal subjects for theoretical epidemiological analyses, which can be used to capture the public's imagination as well as explore scientific principles,

As for a zombie apocalypse, Smith's model shows that a zombie infection would spread quickly (with N representing total population, S the number of susceptible people, Z the zombies, and b the likelihood of transmission). It also shows that zombies would overtake the world— there's no chance for a "stable equilibrium" in which humans could coexist with the undead or eradicate the disease.

Only coordinated attacks against the zombies would save humanity, the model shows.

'WWZ'

Models of disease outbreaks, like the one Smith, developed, play a prominent role in real-life epidemiology, Smith said.

"Unlike most popular monsters, zombies are inherently biological in nature," said Matt Mogk, founder of the Zombie Research Society. "They don't fly or live forever, so you can apply real-world biological models to them."

Zombies are walking representations of a contagion because they depict flesh-devouring monsters who spread their affliction by gnawing on the healthy. Some recent zombie flicks, notably "28 Days Later" and "Zombieland," even explicitly portray zombieism as a virus.

"A zombie is a bit like giving a virus legs and teeth," said Ian MacKay, a virologist at the Australian Infectious Diseases Research Centre, University of Queensland, who blogged about "World War Z." "This is basically a virus taking over a host, and spreading very quickly and efficiently. ... It's an extreme virus-transmission event if you like."

In "World War Z," Brad Pitt plays a U.N. inspector searching the globe for the origin of the zombie outbreak, paralleling the quests of many real-life virus hunters, Mackay said. "Trying to find the index case, or case zero, bears quite a resemblance to conventional epidemiology," Mackay said. The movie is (somewhat loosely) based on Max Brooks' novel of the same name, which included unprecedented, true-to-life detail about the political, medical and sociological ramifications of a zombie outbreak, earning the thriller a spot on a U.S. Naval War College reading list.

Math tackles the hordes

Analyzing zombies adds a couple of new wrinkles to traditional disease modeling, Smith said: Dead people can be resurrected as zombies, and humans will attack the infected. "Usually, the dead aren't a dynamic variable," Smith said. "And people don't try to kill the people who have an infection."

Those elements — infections and attacks on zombies — made the model more complicated, because they introduce two nonlinear factors or factors that don't change at a constant rate, said Smith, who has modeled outbreaks of HIV, malaria and West Nile virus. Most disease models include only one nonlinear element: disease transmission. Having two nonlinear factors makes zombie math extremely sensitive to small changes to parameters, Smith said.

The most important parameter, however, was the infectivity of the zombie disease. In zombie movies, the affliction spreads fast, Mackay said. In "World War Z," for instance, Pitt's character counts out the seconds from bite to zombification, whereas most infections take days, months or even years in the case of HIV to manifest.

That high infectivity makes the zombie epidemic unstoppable in most cases, according to Smith's model. "Because it only takes one zombie to overtake a city," neither quarantine nor a slower disease progression could stop the Zombie Apocalypse — only delay it, did Smith say. Only frequent, increasingly effective attacks against humanity's transformed brethren would win an actual zombie war, he said.

To model that kind of human-zombie tangling, Smith used a relatively new mathematical technique called "impulsive differential equations," which show how abrupt shocks affect systems. Commonly used to model satellite orbits, the technique didn't appear until the 1990s, whereas most mathematical tools date back centuries.

Either way the outlook is grim for the normal people. So you can stand on the sidelines now and do nothing or get ready to kill some flesh biting ,brain nibbling zombified walking undead.

What will it be?

SOMEPLACE TO CALL HOME

Let's face it, when the zombies run wild in the streets and begin to devour your neighbors you are going to want to relocate.

Finding that one right place to call home is not going to be a walk in the park. Searching for the right place to feel safe and allow yourself tie mot process the flesh eating dead will be a relief.

Shelters

Having a place to call home, even temporarily is something that everyone needs during a disaster. When the dead roam the earth it will be even more difficult to find the right place to hang your hat. Learning how to build your own shelter might be the difference between survival against the elements and becoming one of the walking dead.

A shelter can range from a "natural shelter"; such as a cave or a fallen-down tree to an intermediate form of man-made shelters such as a debris hut, a tree pit shelter, or a snow cave, to completely man-made structures such as a tarp, tent, or a longhouse.

Whether you are stranded in the wilderness or preparing for a tornado, a safe place to stay could save your life. In any disaster situation, advance preparation is always more effective than improvisation. Stock your car or basement with emergency supplies now, and learn how to seek shelter before you're forced to.

Pack a one person tent. A lightweight, portable tent takes up little room in your car. Setting one up is much easier and faster than building a shelter from scratch, if you end up lost or caught in a storm.

- This is also a good solution if you may need to leave your home at a moment's notice. Keep food, water, and fuel in the car as well, or in a handheld pack as portable as you can make it.

Types of shelters

When looking for a shelter site, keep in mind the type of shelter (protection) you need. However, you must also consider--

- How much time and effort you need to build the shelter.

- If the shelter will adequately protect you from the elements (sun, wind, rain, and snow).

- If you have the tools to build it. If not, can you make improvised tools?

- If you have the type and amount of materials needed to build it.

To answer these questions, you need to know how to make various types of shelters and what materials you need to make them.

There are many kinds of survival shelters, but this is the easiest, most efficient shelter for most wooded areas; especially coniferous.

Please note that many environments may not provide the resources you need to build this shelter, and that while this practical, easy shelter is applicable to many areas in the United States, (and almost anywhere else with trees) no one shelter is the end all, be all shelter

The ability to build a safe and comfortable shelter quickly in an emergency; without compromising effectiveness is key to survival.

Camping can be a lot of fun and a great way to enjoy nature. Many people enjoy using a tent for the ease at which they can be set up. However, tents can be heavy and bulky to carry with you on a camping trip. To make your camping trip less difficult, you may want to use a tarp shelter. Tarps are lightweight and fairly easy to build a shelter with, helping to make your camping trip a comfortable one.

- Making sure to stretch the tarp tight before staking it. Finish the other corners.

- Don't hammer the stakes in too deeply yet, as you will redo them when you construct the walls of your tent.

- If you don't have stakes, or your tarp doesn't have holes for stakes, use heavy rocks instead to secure it to the ground.

Method part 1

Basic Line Tent

1. Find a flat area. The best areas for building a tarp shelter are places that have flat ground. This can make creating the shelter a bit easier and will allow you a more comfortable place to sleep in. Take some time to find a nice, flat area before building your tarp shelter

2. Look above for dead branches. Once you've found a nice place on the ground for your shelter, you will want to look above it. Dead branches can pose a serious hazard to campers if they are knocked down by wind. Always avoid placing your shelter under any branches that look old, dead, or dangerous to avoid having one fall on you.

3. Create the ridge-line. The ridge-line will support the top section of your tarp shelter. This line is created by stringing a length of cord between two trees. This gives your tarp an elevated point of support and will form the shape of the a-frame tarp shelter. Place the ridge-line using these steps:

- Tie one section of the rope to a tree. Place it as high up the tree trunk as you would like the roof of your tarp shelter to be.
- Bring the other end over to the adjacent tree and tie it at the same level.
- Make sure the cord is as tight as it can be to ensure a strong ridge-line.

4. This ridge-line is created by tying a length of rope tightly between two trees or other points of support. This will create a point that you can secure your tarp to and finish your shelter.

- Tie one end of the rope around the trunk of a tree. Tie it at the height that you want the top of your shelter to be at.

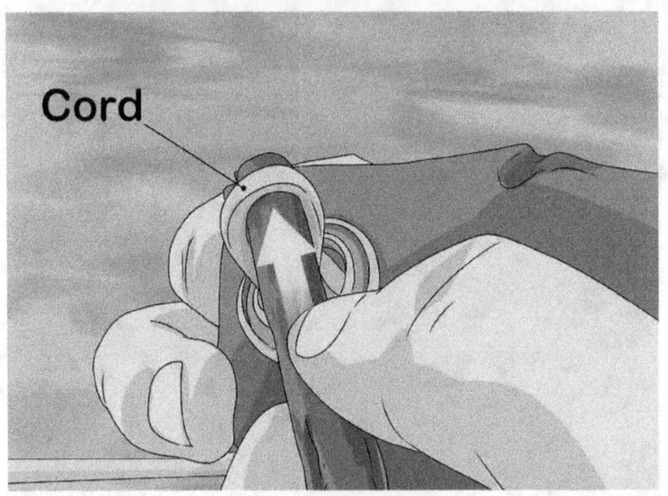

5. Fix one edge of the tarp to the cord. The lean-to tarp shelter requires you to fix one edge of your tarp to your ridge-line. You can attach the tarp to the ridge-line using cord or rope and many tarps will come with grommets or loops built in. Make sure you attach the tarp to the ridge-line tightly to build a strong tarp shelter.

- Your tarp may have holes pre-made along its edge. If so, you can thread the ridge-line through these for an easy way to join them together.
- Many tarps will have loops along the corners or edges that can be used to tie them to your ridge-line.

6. Anchor the tarp to the ground. Once the top edge has been tied to the ridge-line, you can secure the bottom edge of the lean-to tarp shelter. Pull the bottom edge away from the center until it is at an angle that you want. Place anchoring stakes in the ground at the corners of the tarp and tie the tarp to them. This will hold the bottom portion of your shelter securely in place.

- Most people recommend using a 45 degree angle for their lean-to.
- Try adjusting the angle to raise or lower the height of the shelter's "ceiling".

For additional protection from wind and rain, place some brush, your rucksack, or other equipment at the sides of the lean-to.

To reduce heat loss to the ground, place some type of insulating material, such as leaves or pine needles, inside your lean-to.

Note: When at rest, you lose as much as 80 percent of your body heat to the ground.

To increase your security from enemy observation, lower the lean-to's silhouette by making two changes. First, secure the support lines to the trees at knee height (not at waist height) using two knee-high sticks in the two center grommets (sides of a lean-to). Second, angle the poncho to the ground, securing it with sharpened sticks, as above.

7. Lay the tarp over the rope. Once your ridge-line has been created, you can lay the tarp over top of it. For an a-frame tarp shelter, place the tarp over the ridge-line in the center of the tarp. This will leave equal halves of the tarp hanging down from the ridge-line.

• Make sure the tarp is equally hanging from both sides of the ridge-line to avoid problems.

8. Anchor the tarp to the ground. After you've placed the tarp over the ridge-line, you can fasten it to the ground. Take one of the bottom sections of tarp and pull it outwards, away from the center of the tent. Once you've gotten it to a place that you like, secure it to the ground by taking these steps:

- Place a tent stake into the ground, near to the point the tarps corner while it is stretched out.
- Tie a length of cord between the tent stake and the corner of the tarp.
- Make sure this cord is tight and holds the tarp securely to the ground.
- Do the same thing for each of the other three corners of your a-frame tarp shelter.

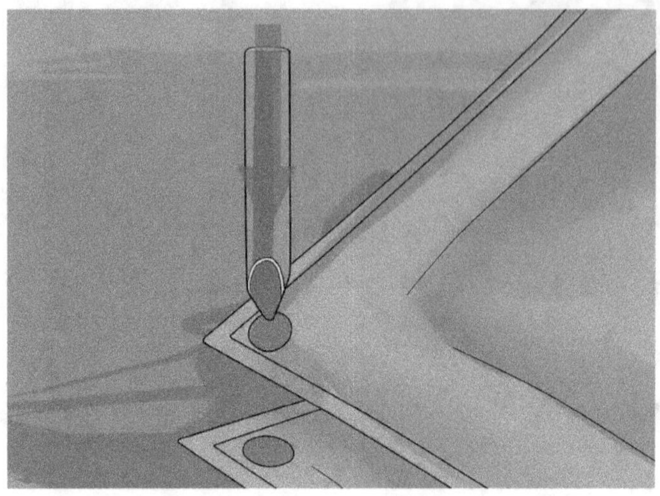

9. Secure the walls to the ground. If you've secured the first tarp with stakes, remove one stake, then line up the holes in the two tarps, and hammer the stake back into the ground. Repeat with the other corners one by one. If you've secured the first tarp with rocks, just lift each rock and place the corners of the wall tarp under them so that the rocks hold both tarps in place.

10. Build embankments to keep out water, if necessary. If you're worried about potential rain flooding your tent, you can keep out water with rocks and dirt. Just use whatever you can find around you, sticks, rocks, and dirt, to build a small wall around your tent's floor tarp.

• Alternatively, if your tent is on a slope, you can dig trenches around both sides of your tent using a small shovel or a sharp rock, which will help rain flow around your tent instead of into it.

Troubleshooting Common Problems

1. Make a tent with one large tarp. If you don't have two tarps, but the one you have is large enough, you can make a tent with floor and roof with the single tarp. Lay the tarp on the ground beneath the rope. Place two rocks on two corners, and two rocks in the center of the tarp at the edges. Throw the edge of the tarp not held down over the rope, and then secure that edge right on top of the opposite edge of the tarp with the same rocks.

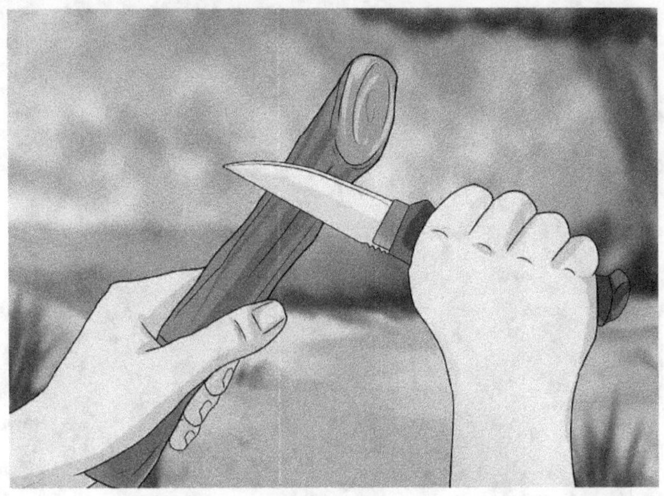

2. Carve stakes out of broken branches. If you want to secure your tent with stakes but you don't have any with you, you can use broken tree branches. Take a knife and whittle one end of four branches down to a point.

- You'll need to find branches that are thin enough to fit through the stake holes in the tarps but thick enough to not break. If you can snap it easily with your hands it's probably not strong enough.

3. Make a tent with only one tree. If you can't find two trees that are a good distance apart, you can make a tent of a different shape with one tree. You'll need stakes and a tarp with holes for stakes for this method. Using your rope, tie one corner of the tarp to the tree. Then just stretch out the tarp and stake the other corners into the ground.

- If you have another tarp you can stake it to the ground beneath the roof tarp. Use the same stakes and drive them through both tarps, with the corners lined up. Then take one more stake to secure the corner of the floor tarp that is closest to the tree.

Method 2

Three-Pole Parachute Tepee

If you have a parachute and three – six poles and the tactical situation allows, make a parachute tepee. It is easy and takes very little time to make this tepee. It provides protection from the elements and can act as a signaling device by enhancing a small amount of light from a fire or candle. It is large enough to hold several people and their equipment and to allow sleeping, cooking, and storing firewood.

You can make this tepee using parts of or a whole personnel main or reserve parachute canopy. If using a standard personnel parachute, you need three poles 3.5 to 4.5 meters long and about 5 centimeters in diameter.

To make this tepee --

• Lay the poles on the ground and lash them together at one end.

• Stand the framework up and spread the poles to form a tripod.

• For more support, place additional poles against the tripod. Five or six additional poles work best, but do not lash them to the tripod.

•   Determine the wind direction and locate the entrance 90 degrees or more from the mean wind direction.

•   Lay out the parachute on the "backside" of the poles and locate the bridle loop (nylon web loop) at the top (apex) of the canopy.

- Place the bridle loop over the top of a free-standing pole. Then place the pole back up against the grouping of poles so that the canopy's apex is at the same height as the lashing on the poles.

- Wrap the canopy around one side of the tripod. The canopy should be of double thickness, as you are wrapping an entire parachute. You need only wrap half of the tripod, as the remainder of the canopy will encircle the pole in the opposite direction.

- Construct the entrance by wrapping the folded edges of the canopy around two free-standing poles. You can then place the poles side by side to close the tepee's entrance.

- Place all extra canopy underneath the tepee poles and inside to create a floor for the shelter.

- Leave a 30- to a 50-centimeter opening at the top for ventilation if you intend to have a fire inside the tepee.

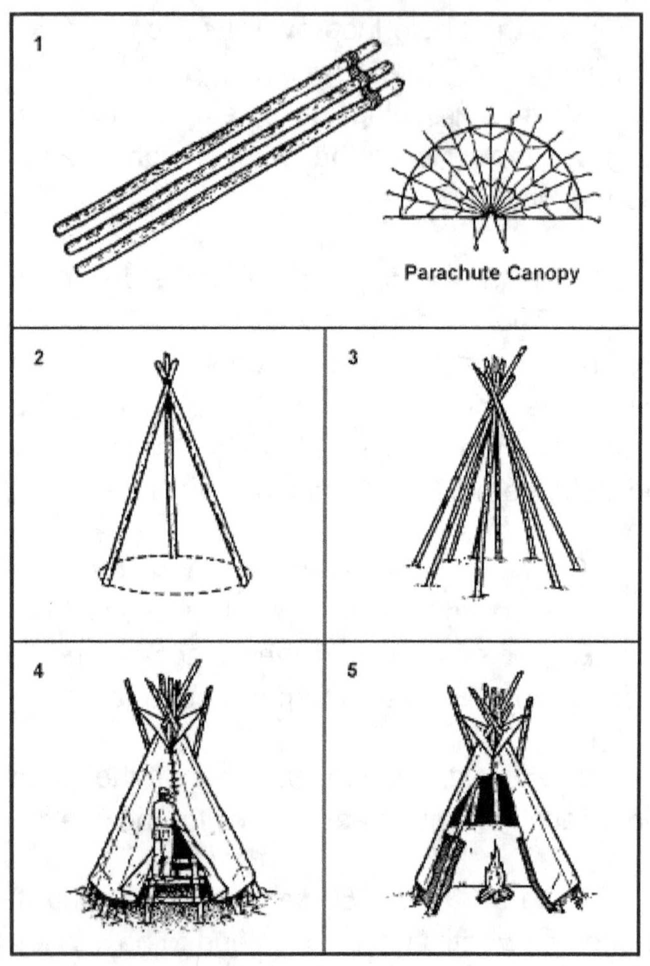

1
Parachute Canopy
2
3
4
5

Method 3

No-Pole Parachute Tepee

You use the same materials, except for the center pole, as for the one-pole parachute tepee.

To make this tepee

• Tie a line to the top of parachute material with a previously cut suspension line.

• Throw the line over a tree limb, and tie it to the tree trunk.

• Starting at the opposite side from the door, emplace a stake on the scribed 3.5- to 4.3-meter circle.

• Tie the first line on the lower lateral band.

• Continue emplacing the stakes and tying the lines to them.

• After staking down the material, unfasten the line tied to the tree trunk, tighten the tepee material by pulling on this line, and tie it securely to the tree trunk.

Method 4

One-Man Shelter

A one-man shelter you can easily make using a parachute requires a tree and three poles. One pole should be about 4.5 meters long and the other two about 3 meters long.

To make this shelter --

•   Secure the 4.5-meter pole to the tree at about waist height.

•   Lay the two 3-meter poles on the ground on either side of and in the same direction as the 4.5-meter pole.

•   Lay the folded canopy over the 4.5-meter pole so that about the same amount of material hangs on both sides.

•   Tuck the excess material under the 3-meter poles, and spread it on the ground inside to serve as a floor.

•   Stake down or put a spreader between the two 3-meter poles at the shelter's entrance so they will not slide inward.

•   Use any excess material to cover the entrance.

The parachute cloth makes this shelter wind resistant, and the shelter is small enough that it is easily warmed. A candle, used carefully, can keep the inside temperature comfortable. This shelter is unsatisfactory, however, when snow is falling as even a light snowfall will cave it in.

Method 5

Field-Expedient Lean-To

If you are in a wooded area and have enough natural materials, you can make a field-expedient lean-to without the aid of tools or with only a knife. It takes longer to make this type of shelter than it does to make other types, but it will protect you from the elements.

You will need two trees (or upright poles) about 2 meters apart; one pole about 2 meters long and 2.5 centimeters in diameter; five to eight poles about 3 meters long and 2.5 centimeters in diameter for beams; cord or vines for securing the horizontal support to the trees; and other poles, saplings, or vines to crisscross the beams.

To make this lean-to--

• Tie the 2-meter pole to the two trees at the waist to chest height. This is the horizontal support. If a standing tree is not available, construct a biped using Y-shaped sticks or two tripods.

• Place one end of the beams (3-meter poles) on one side of the horizontal support. As with all lean-to type shelters, be sure to place the lean-to's backside into the wind.

• Crisscross saplings or vines on the beams.

• Cover the framework with brush, leaves, pine needles, or grass, starting at the bottom and working your way up like shingling.

• Place straw, leaves, pine needles, or grass inside the shelter for bedding.

In cold weather, add to your lean-to's comfort by building a fire reflector wall. Drive four 1.5-meter-long stakes into the ground to support the wall. Stack green logs on top of one another between the support stakes. Form two rows of stacked logs to create an inner space within the wall that you can fill with dirt. This action not only strengthens the wall but makes it more heat reflective. Bind the top of the support stakes so that the green logs and dirt will stay in place.

With just a little more effort you can have a drying rack. Cut a few 2-centimeter-diameter poles (length depends on the distance between the lean-to's horizontal support and the top of the fire reflector wall). Lay one end of the poles on the lean-to support and the other end on top of the reflector wall. Place and tie into place smaller sticks across these poles. You now have a place to dry clothes, meat, or fish.

Method 6

Swamp Bed

In a marsh or swamp, or any area with standing water or continually wet ground, the swamp bed keeps you out of the water. When selecting such a site, consider the weather, wind, tides, and available materials.

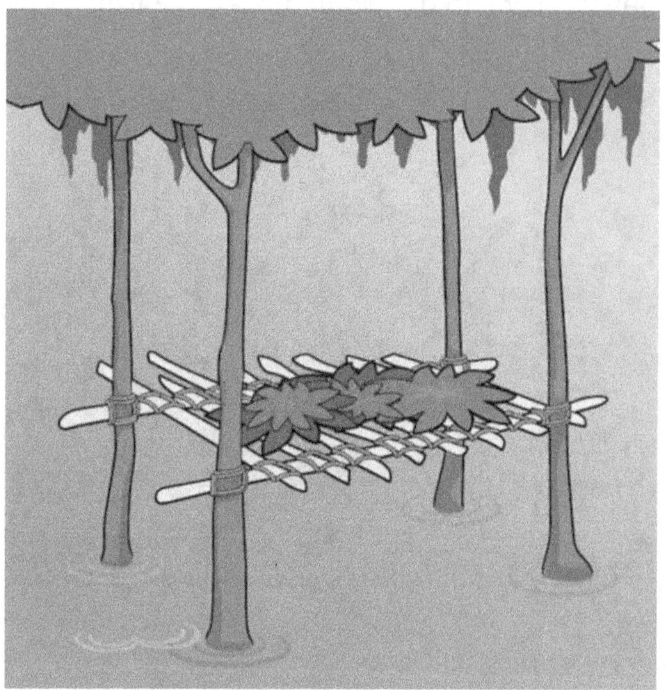

To make a swamp bed—

• Look for four trees clustered in a rectangle, or cut four poles (bamboo is ideal) and drive them firmly into the ground so they form a rectangle. They should be far enough apart and strong enough to support your height and weight, to include equipment.

• Cut two poles that span the width of the rectangle. They, too, must be strong enough to support your weight.

• Secure these two poles to the trees (or poles). Be sure they are high enough above the ground or water to allow for tides and high water.

• Cut additional poles that span the rectangle's length. Lay them across the two side poles, and secure them.

• Cover the top of the bed frame with broad leaves or grass to form a soft sleeping surface.

• Build a fire pad by laying clay, silt, or mud on one comer of the swamp bed and allow it to dry.

Another shelter designed to get you above and out of the water or wet ground uses the same rectangular configuration as the swamp bed. You very simply lay sticks and branches lengthwise on the inside of the trees (or poles) until there is enough material to raise the sleeping surface above the water level.

Natural Shelters

Do not overlook natural formations that provide shelter. Examples are caves, rocky crevices, clumps of bushes, small depressions, large rocks on leeward sides of hills, large trees with low-hanging limbs, and fallen trees with thick branches. However, when selecting a natural formation--

• Stay away from the low ground such as ravines, narrow valleys, or creek beds. Low areas collect the heavy cold air at night and are therefore colder than the surrounding high ground. Thick, brushy, low ground also harbors more insects.

• Check for poisonous snakes, ticks, mites, scorpions, and stinging ants.

• Look for loose rocks, dead limbs, coconuts, or other natural growth that could fall on your shelter.

Method 7

Debris Hut

For warmth and ease of construction, this shelter is one of the best. When a shelter is essential to survival, build this shelter.

To make a debris hut

• Build it by making a tripod with two short stakes and a long ridgepole or by placing one end of a long ridgepole on top of a sturdy base.

• Secure the ridgepole (pole running the length of the shelter) using the tripod method or by anchoring it to a tree at about waist height.

• Prop large sticks along both sides of the ridgepole to create a wedge-shaped ribbing effect. Ensure the ribbing is wide enough to accommodate your body and steep enough to shed moisture.

• Place finer sticks and brush crosswise on the ribbing. These form a latticework that will keep the insulating material (grass, pine needles, and leaves) from falling through the ribbing into the sleeping area.

• Add light, dry, if possible, soft debris over the ribbing until the insulating material is at least 1 meter thick--the thicker the better.

• Place a 30-centimeter layer of insulating material inside the shelter.

• At the entrance, pile insulating material that you can drag to you once inside the shelter to close the entrance or build a door.

• As a final step in constructing this shelter, add shingling material or branches on top of the debris layer to prevent the insulating material from blowing away in a storm.

Method 8

Tree-Pit Snow Shelter

If you are in a cold, snow-covered area where evergreen trees grow and you have a digging tool, you can make a tree-pit shelter

To make this shelter--

• Find a tree with bushy branches that provide overhead cover.

• Dig out the snow around the tree trunk until you reach the depth and diameter you desire, or until you reach the ground.

• Pack the snow around the top and the inside of the hole to provide support.

• Find and cut other evergreen boughs. Place them over the top of the pit to give you additional overhead cover. Place evergreen boughs in the bottom of the pit for insulation.

Building a shelter can make the largest difference in your survival. Keeping the elements out and keeping you warm is a primary concern but also allowing yourself to have some momentary solace from the attacking dead is also just as important. Keeping the zombies out and you in a safe location is the break you will need to continue on your way through this apocalyptic world.

Learning to take time out from all the beheading and brain smashing on the undead walkers is paramount to your mental health as well. One can only take so much bloodletting before it warps your own sense of right and wrong. Shelters can be that place to just get away in privacy to allow that needed shut eye and repair rom the carnage that you have suffered through. Zombies are so stressful.

What do you need to do to protect my family and home from zombies?" Well look no further, here are 10 simple ways to help you prepare for a zombie attack and create a zombie proof home.

Build your home in a remote area: on a mountain, in the woods, in the desert or on the moon like MJ did. Zombies concentrate in areas with large human populations since human flesh is their source of sentience, so living in a remote area with few inhabitants with increase your chances of survival.

2. Tall Fences: Building a tall smooth surfaced fence will prevent zombies from entering your property. Muscle tissue deteriorates in the transformation process rendering zombies incapable of scaling walls.

3. Pit traps: Dig several large holes in the ground and cover them with big tree branches and leaves. If a zombie finds a way to breach your perimeter, the pit trap will provide the same defense as the tall fence.

4. Build all doors out of solid wood or metal: Zombies do not have a great deal of strength due to the muscle deterioration as mentioned above. The strength of a zombie will be no match against a well enforced door. Windows

should also be reinforced in the event of a zombie invasion.

5. Well water vs. public water: Have a well on your property, in the event of a zombie outbreak you cannot rely on public water supply. The workers at your local water treatment facility might be zombies and everyone knows that zombies have absolutely no work ethic.

6. Generators and fuel: Knowing the work ethics of zombies, or lack thereof, it is best to have a generator at your residence in order to maintain your preferred quality of life. A hearty supply of fuel will be needed as well to insure continued use of your generator.

7. Sound diversions: Zombies have an acute sense of hearing. If your property is large enough, install speakers at the perimeter of your property. If a perimeter breech occurs play loud sounds to lure the zombies away from your home and loved ones. Your generator will come in handy here.

8. Weapons: If you find that you have no other choice but to fight, a sharp long machete or a scythe are good weapons of choice as you will be able to maintain a distance whilst decapitating your undead assailants.

9. Own a mobile home: The best way to evade a zombie attack is to constantly be on the move. A mobile home is a good option as it allows you to flee from an attack of the undead without sacrificing the comforts of home.

10. If you can't beat them, join them: You might end up eating your first born but at least you won't have to pay for their college tuition.

LOCATION, LOCATION, LOCATION

When the Zombie outbreak happens and the apocalypse is upon us there are a few things to note. Survival will be assuredly better if you have a safe place to go when it all comes down.

When it comes to the zombie apocalypse it is just like real estate. Location, Location, Location is key.

Knowing where to go and not to go is key to survival in the zombie filled future as we know it. Here are a few dos and don'ts for the end times.

The safest place to hide would be in the arctic tundra because zombies would have trouble moving in the snow, the fierce winds would throw them off your scent, and they actually have a possibility of freezing in their tracks while you hide in a safe cave with your supplies. Also, it is very remote and they wouldn't really go there unless they were following you.

Imagine: The Zombie Apocalypse is here. You try to wait it out in your home, but that option is no good. Your community is overrun with the undead. You grab your gear and head out. But where do you go? Where is the best place to set up a defensive position and ride out the storm?

According to the Zombie Emergency Tactical Agency, here are the best places to hide out (or a bug in) during the zombie apocalypse.

Mountains

Mountains come in at number 5. Sure, you will be in the woods, unsupported, without any real manmade defenses between you and the undead. But think logically here. Zombies, at least the majority of them, are going to be attracted to the large metropolitan areas. Of course, the largest number of infected will probably be in large cities, but when those zombies go out looking for brains to munch on, chances are they will wander the streets close to home, or towards other large cities. The chances of them coming to the mountains are minimal.

Also, the mountains form a natural defense and resources for possible long-term survival. If you select a ridgeline upon which to set up camp, you will be able to see anyone or anything approaching from quite a distance off – zombies or not. With the right camp, you could have fresh water, plenty of fish and game, and have time to set up other constructed defenses, such as sharpened spikes and wooden fences, pitfalls for the undead, and more.

Low temperatures might be helpful to disable the undead, but also are places where the shortage of food would represent a problem. In any case, high mountains are mostly uninhabited so that would mean the possibility to live while the zombie problem spreads in different areas.

Islands

Islands come in at number 2 for all the logical reasons. Zombies, to our knowledge, do not know how to drive boats. However, they can still swim (some of them). However, an island is a great natural defense. You can see anything approaching the island from miles away, and take the needed precautions. It should be simple enough to pick off the wandering zombie who decides to swim ashore on your island.

There are some downsides, like food shortages and (depending on the location) fresh water supply. However, with a little planning, you can easily find the perfect island ahead of time and have a plan. Plus, the scenery is beautiful. You can always keep your boat handy, and in good condition, for supply runs back to shore as well. It's not like the undead is going to steal your boat. Also, similar to the mountains, chances are zombies will not go swimming out to sea to hunt for human brains.

If you are looking for the ultimate escape from the zombie carnage, you should be searching for a far civilization inhabited island. That is your best option since you would have food, water, and also a place to build your home. Some islands even offer you only one entrance and the best part is that there are still many islands not touched by the hand of man, so you have plenty to choose.

Prisons

Prisons are an ok place to hide out in too. They are, of course, designed to keep people in, which in turn, can be used to help keep people out. The razor wire and fences that surround most prisons will do a nice job of keeping out the lone zombie, but once you have hordes storming the prison, you could have a problem.

Make sure if you do choose a prison as your location, you quickly lock down and fortify the transport area of the prison. This is where the police drop off and pick up prisoners. From the inside, it is difficult to get out this way – but from the outside trying to come in, it is an obvious weak point. Make sure to fix that.

The downsides are, well, you are in a prison. You will have to make supply runs outside of the prison in order to keep food and fresh water on hand. However, the fortification a prison provides in the wake of a zombie outbreak can be quite comforting. You may have to risk life and limb to run out for supplies, but you will feel very safe and sound when you return back to your camp.

Jails are supposed to be safe, so you should give them a try. Many people can be staying there, and if they are big enough you won't be worrying about privacy. The real problem during the outbreak is to make the prisoners vacate. Who's going to enter first and let the inmates out? Albeit if you look for the minimal security complex in Norway you'll be staying in a luxury hotel but that would be no help containing the undead.

Castles

Castles are a great choice for a million reasons. They are designed to withstand attacks, they are usually comfortable living, most have their own well for fresh water, and so much more. If you are in close proximity to a castle during the zombie apocalypse, this is the place to go. Setting up defenses could be easy. Also, to boot, a lot of castles are also built in locations using the best of the environment and the natural defenses around it.

Of course, zombies most likely will not come running up to a castle looking for blood. If the castle is not in the middle of the city, you should be fine with the number of zombies that attack your position. Just remember most castles are large, which means a good amount of upkeep. This location might be best suited for a team of survivors instead of one lone wolf. Still, though, this location comes in at almost the top of our list. Find yourself a castle with modern security upgrades and in good working order, and you're set for the long haul.

History is always wise, if castles served their purpose to let people protect themselves from hordes of enemies thirsting for blood, these places would do the same even if the threat is now of an undead kind. Some castles are just like big fortified farms, so you would be saving time in building the walls and using it planting some food instead.

Military Base

Old forts are in our opinion, the best option. First of all, they are literally built for defensive posturing. This means if you can find a fort that has withstood the test of time, these old military outposts are the primo option for a defensive position. Some forts are close to the water as well, which helps to provide a natural choke point for the zombie attacks. Better still, most forts are on the outskirts of towns and cities, meaning the population around them is relatively low. Therefore, the zombie population is as well.

Make sure to bring plenty of supplies, and be prepared for supply runs for sure. But still – a military designed fortified location built specifically for defense? This seems like a no-brainer. Get you (and your team) to this location, and you won't have anything to worry about. Zombies, other people, vehicles, even attack ships stand to lose the battle if they come after you. Add in a couple of modern-day defense systems, or take over a modern-day fort – and you are ready to roll for the long haul.

Any of these locations will do. Just remember, it is best to have a plan before the zombie apocalypse occurs. Don't wait until the last minute to make a plan, or you could easily become one of the roaming undead.

Similar to the missile silo, the military bases are good hiding places (if you love to eat canned foods). You would have lots of ammo and guns to protect the perimeter, and hopefully you would be mostly out of range if the base is placed far from civilization. Anyway you should be aware that people don't get crazy with the guns or you'll be facing a bigger problem than zombies, enraged people with guns.

Same as a military installation the missile silo is a great discovery to hide yourself away from the zombie terror.

Similar to a bunker, the missile silo provides the perfect place to hide, several floors on the underground and a secure perimeter. All silos are well fortified and placed in natural areas where little to no human beings are living. As some of them are packaged to serve as houses for scientists and militaries, these may have beds and food. Just make sure that missiles are in optimum conditions or search for an abandoned missile silo instead.

Bank

A bank could be a good temporary place to hide for a few days. Most of the banks have one strong entrance and can be electronically sealed. Banks used to be fully monitored by cameras and for extreme safety you can sleep in the main vault. However, this should be only an immediate option before leaving town. All banks are placed on populated areas and you would have to go out searching for food from time to time, since we haven't figured out any receipt with money as its main ingredient.

Mountain Mine

A mine could be a good place to hide during the outbreak. You should have control over all the entrances to make it safe. Abandoned mines can bring additional dangers. Some mines actually have air filters and water purifiers, so you won't have to worry about that. A strategic mine should be located in a low-dense populated area, far from urbanistic complexes and near to self-sustainable food sources like farms. You would have to go out during the days to collect food, but anyhow if you are near the fields you can plant food by your own means.

Natural Cave

Similar to mountain mines, these would provide safe places to hide, especially if they are fully explored. However like in the previous case, entrances will have to be fortified, and most important, you will have to watch out that the cave you choose is not the actual household of an enraged bear.

Lighthouse

A lighthouse indeed is a safe place, surrounded by water and with a high point that gives you a panoramic view. It still has the limitation of space, so you better choose friendly companions to hide there with you. However it can be a good alternative during the nights, unless zombies learn how to swim (I hope they don't), you won't be worrying too much about security.

Ship

This is one of the best alternatives to scape-hide during a zombie outbreak. You will be out of reach from all the flesh eaters in ground Some ships have water desalinization devices. You would only have to descend to earth from time to time in order to collect food. Alternatively, you will be able to search for safe inhabited places. But be aware you are not travelling with infected passengers.

Safe Houses

Some modern houses are built with special features that make them true fortresses. Fully automated to be sealed with metal coverage for windows and doors, safe houses represent the new expression of being prepared for the worst possible situation. Although these might be expensive, you can take someone else's safe house if he/she was not fortunate to reach it in time.

Farm

Build four walls to secure the perimeter and you got it, the safest place to be. Choose a farm with a source of water, a pit maybe. Farms are located far from the cities and that makes them excellent places to be during the outbreak. The eventual casualties would be considerably low and you won't be worrying about going out for food.

Sea platforms for Oil Extraction

These man-made islands are far from coast and are nearly indestructible. If you are passionate about fishing, then this would be the best option. Live like a sailor in the middle of the sea and never worry again about the zombies, even if they learn how to swim there are few ways to enter into these constructions, some are only reachable by air and are suspended above the water level.

The worst places to go when zombies attack.

Hiding in a loft/attic

There is often only one way in and out, so you are pretty much trapped.

Shopping centers/malls

This was a popular attraction before the living became the undead, so it's only natural to assume that a lot of undead people would end up here. After all they are in search of living people and this is where everyone would expect to find them.

Crowded cities

This is the area where the most living once resided, so it's only natural that it's going to be full of zombies, and what do zombies want to do? EAT YOU!

Supermarkets

These are extremely dangerous places to go because they have too many walls and shelves blocking your view. So you will be unable to see those zombies lurking around the corners. The areas are very compact so you can easily get blocked in by 10-15 zombies.

Rooftops

These can be your best or worst friend. They are the best place if you use them correctly, although they can leave you trapped and unable to get away from the zombies who are preparing for a feast. Even if the zombies can't make it on the roof you could still be in real trouble; zombies are really persistent and will crowd around the roof leaving you unable to get down.

Sporting Goods Stores

Many people's first instinct when a zombie apocalypse breaks out would be to go to a sporting goods store. These places are full of guns, crossbows, and plenty of other weapons that they need to protect themselves. Unfortunately, since so many other people will have the same idea, you will likely end up in a confrontation with a crazy person who is fighting to survive. In the end, you could end up getting killed by a living person with a gun rather than a zombie.

Amusement Parks

Amusement parks are really fun if the world hasn't come to an end, however, during a zombie apocalypse, these aren't the best places to hide. There isn't much shelter or places to hide in an amusement park. There are also plenty of places to get cornered by a zombie or a herd of zombies. You also don't want to be at an amusement park right when the virus first breaks out because amusement parks are known to be the most germ infested areas you can be in.

A Brain Museum

There are brain museums all around the world that are open to the public. There are thousands of actual brains that were once in human heads in these museums that are on display to show people the effects that certain psychological and physical conditions have on the brain. If zombies have a good sense of smell, a brain museum would be like a candy store for them. Just being around thousands of brains will drive zombies within a 10 mile radius, crazy.

Hospitals

Of the 10 worst place to hide during zombie apocalypse, this is by far the worst. You may think that the hospital is the best place to go during a zombie apocalypse, but you would be wrong. First of all, patient 0 could have been a patient at the hospital and there could be zombies walking around everywhere. Next, before people try to get to remote areas to hide, they are going to need medical supplies just in case something were to happen. These people will likely head to the hospital armed. If you encounter one of these people, you could be in trouble. Finally, drug addicts will be more worried about getting their fix than saving themselves. This could lead to a deadly situation.

Sewers

Sewers may sound like a good place to hide because you are underground, away from the zombies. In reality, these aren't the best places to hide. Not only are they dirty and cramped, you could go crazy after a while without seeing the sun. Also, you would have no access to any food or clean water. Also, you would likely need to share your space with diseases rats. Finally, if zombies did make there way into the sewers, you wouldn't have an easy way to escape.

The Subway

There are several reasons to avoid a subway. First, during the initial outbreak, millions of people will be flocking to the subway to get out of the city. This can turn the subway into the area that is the most highly populated by zombies. Next, subways are usually found in only big cities, which is were the problem will be the worst. Finally, when the subway breaks down and there are thousands of people trapped, a riot can ensure and you might not make it out alive.

HIDE IN THESE PLACES:

1. Office buildings- Many of the same rules regarding apartment houses can be applied to office buildings. Once the first floor has been abandoned, the staircases destroyed, and the elevators shut down, an office building can be a tower of safety.

2. Schools- Unfortunately for our society but fortunately for a zombie siege, inner-city schools have taken on a fortress-like atmosphere. Not only are the buildings themselves built to withstand a riot, but chain-link fences surrounding them make these halls of education look more like military compounds. Food and medical supplies should be readily available from the cafeteria or nurse's office. Often, a school is your best bet- perhaps not for education, but certainly for an undead attack.

However, if you want to hide in your own home, choose one of these hiding places:

1. Retrieve a ladder, climb onto the roof and pull the ladder up next to you. Zombies can't climb, so don't worry about the chimney.

2. Climb up the stairs and destroy them. Don't use fire to burn them down. Many have tried, and either ended up burning their entire house down or catching themselves on fire.

DON'T HIDE IN THESE PLACES:

1. Hospitals: what might seem like the safest, most logical places to hide is actually the worst. Yes, hospitals may be stocked with food, medical supplies, and an expert staff. Yes, the structures themselves could be secured, as with any office or apartment building. Yes, they may have security, even a regular police presence. In any other disaster, a hospital should be your first haven. Not so when the dead rise. Humans with bites or newly murdered corpses are always brought to the hospital. Not good

2. Police stations: the reason to avoid these is fewer zombies, more humans. In all probability, the people living in your city or town will flock to the local police station, creating a nexus of chaos, bodies, and eventual blood. Imagine a packed, writhing crowd of frightened people, too many to control, all trying to force their way into the building they think best represents safety. When the dead rise, locate your local police station- and head the other way.

NOTE: DO NOT go in the mall! It would be so crowded with people looting, hiding, and running to the place they think has the best supply of stock and protection. You might as well be sending up two thousand flares to zombies that say: Hey, I'm a tender, juicy human! Come eat me!

SAFE AND WARM?

Let's face it when the zombie apocalypse does make its way to your neighborhood and you have bugged out. Eventually you will find a place to rest build a shelter and be ready to plan your next move. In the meantime you will want and need to keep warm and dry. This leads us to the next objective which is to make a fire.

Fire is man's best creation and the only way that humans as a race have survived. The use of fire not only for warmth but to cook food, purify water and even clean wounds is in its nature, life sustaining.

Learning the necessary skills to build and make a fire is the cornerstone to keeping you and your loved ones alive as well as warm. There are more than the undead to worry about when you are out in the wild. Beast of all kinds will be just as curious about the taste of your flesh (or food leftovers). Fire is a natural protectant against such beast. It will keep them at bay while allowing you to contemplate your next move.

Honing the skills that you will need to start a fire from natural materials around you will be a true test of skill and patience.

Fire

Making fire is recognized in the sources as significantly increasing the ability to survive physically and mentally. Lighting a fire without a lighter or matches, e.g. by using natural flint and steel with tinder, is a frequent subject of both books on survival and in survival courses. There is an emphasis placed on practicing fire-making skills before venturing into the wilderness. Producing fire under adverse conditions has been made much easier by the introduction of tools such as the solar spark lighter and the fire piston.

Fire is presented as a tool for meeting many survival needs. The heat provided by a fire warms the body, dries wet clothes, disinfects water, and cooks food. Not to be overlooked is the psychological boost and the sense of safety and protection it gives. In the wild, fire can provide a sensation of home, a focal point, in addition to being an essential energy source. Fire may deter wild animals from interfering with a survivor, however, wild animals may be attracted to the light and heat of a fire.

Being able to start a fire is an essential tool for surviving in the wilderness. When someone in your camping group drops the matches into the river or the lighter gets lost along the way, you may need to know how to start a fire using natural or household objects to create friction or magnify the sun.

Learn how to start a fire without using matches or a lighter by reading the methods below.

Method 1

Getting Started

1. Learn how to make tinder for a fire and have your tinder nest ready. For all of the methods below, you will need a tinder nest to nurture the sparks and/or embers you create into a flame.

2. Gather dry wood. In order to create friction and maintain a flame, you will need to use dry wood, as best as you can get.

- Dry wood hiding places. If the area is damp, you may have to check the interior of logs, under ledges, and other places that are protected from wetness.

- Know your trees. Not all wood ignites equally. Depending on your locality, some particular trees start fires more readily. For instance, paper birch yields paper-like bark that, even when wet, often makes an excellent tinder.

- Look beyond wood. Although fire-building is usually taught in the spirit of building a fire in the wilderness, you may have to adapt. In an urban situation there may be no trees, so you may have to look at things like old books, wooden pallets, furniture, and the like to get a fire started.

Method 2

Using Batteries and Steel Wool

1. Find a battery and locate the battery terminals. The terminals are the two circular receiving prongs located on the top of the battery. Any battery voltage will work, but 9-volt batteries will ignite the quickest.

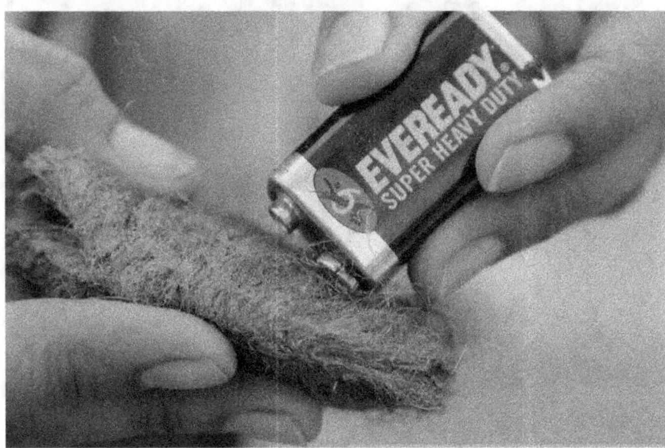

2. Take your steel wool and rub it on the battery terminals. The finer the steel wool, the better for this process.

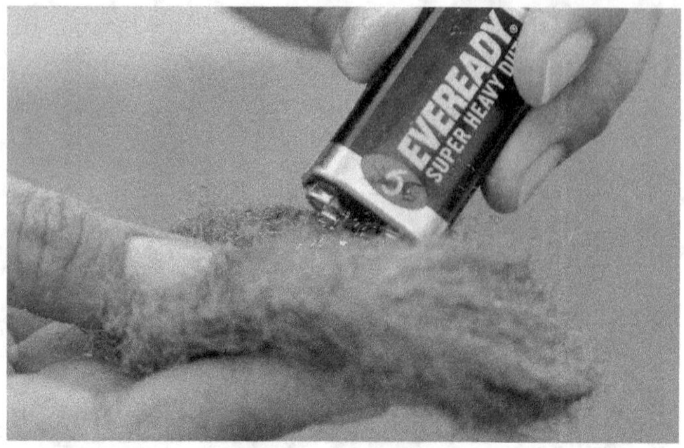

3. Continue to create friction by rubbing the steel wool on the batteries. This process works by creating a current through the tiny steel wires that then heat up and ignite. Another way to do this is rub a paperclip on the battery terminals.

4. Blow gently on the steel wool as it starts to glow. This helps nurture the flame and encourages it to spread.

5. Once the steel wool is glowing brightly, transfer the steel wool to your tinder nest quickly, continuing to blow lightly on the nest until the tinder ignites, creating a flame.

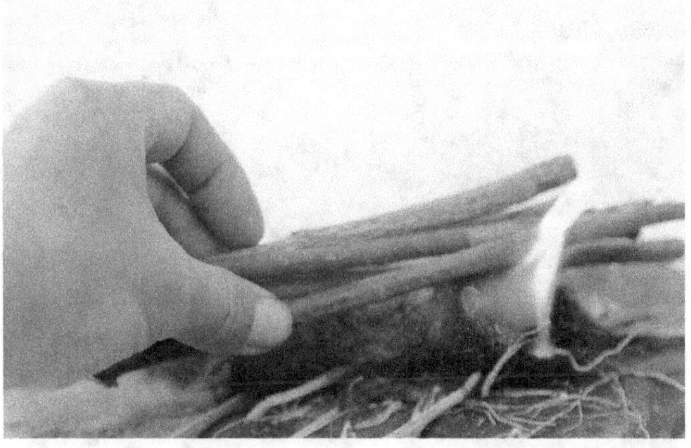

6. Add increasingly larger pieces of dry wood to build your fire once the tinder nest has ignited into a flame zand enjoy your fire!

Method 3

Using Flint and Steel

1. Take your flint rock (a rock that emits sparks) and hold it between your thumb and forefinger. Allow about two or three inches of flint to extend past your grasp.

2. Grab a piece of char cloth between your thumb and the flint. If you do not have any char cloth on hand, you can also use lightweight tree fungus.

3. Take the back of a steel striker or the back of a knife blade (depending on which you have handy) and quickly scrape the steel against the flint. Continue to strike until sparks begin to form.

4. Catch the sparks with your char cloth and continue the process until the cloth glows like an ember. Char cloths are specially designed to hold a glow without catching fire.

5. Transfer the glowing char cloth to your tinder nest and gently blow on it to induce a flame.

6. Begin to add increasingly larger pieces of wood to grow your flame into a fire.

Method 4

Using a Magnifying Glass

1. Notice whether or not there is enough sunlight to create a fire using this method. You generally need the sun to be unobstructed by clouds in order to utilize it with your magnifying glass.

- If you do not have a magnifying glass, eye glass lenses and binocular lenses work as well.
- Adding water to the lens allows you to create a more intense, focused beam of light.
- Tilt the lens toward the sun until the lens creates a small circle of focused light on the tinder nest. You'll probably have to test out holding the lens at different angles to create the most focused beam of light possible.

2. Hold the lens in place until the tinder begins to smoke and flame. Blow lightly on the tinder nest to nurture the flame.

3. Begin to add increasingly larger pieces of dry wood to your tinder nest to create the fire size you desire.

Method 5

Fashioning a Hand Drill

1. Build a tinder nest out of any dry plant material. Again, be sure that the material can catch fire easily.

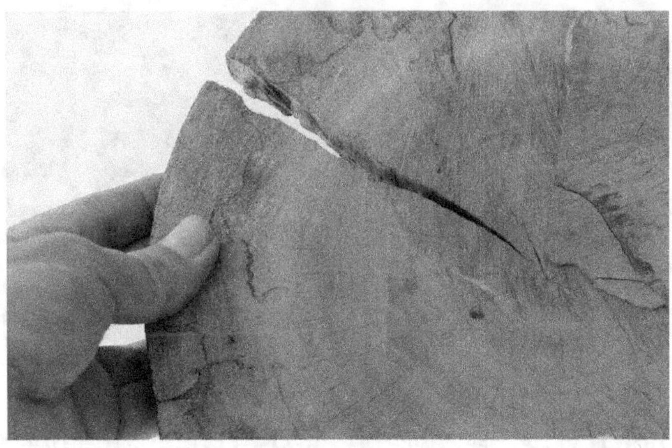

2. Find a piece of wood to use as the base of your hand drill, otherwise known as a fire board. You will drill on this wood piece to create friction.

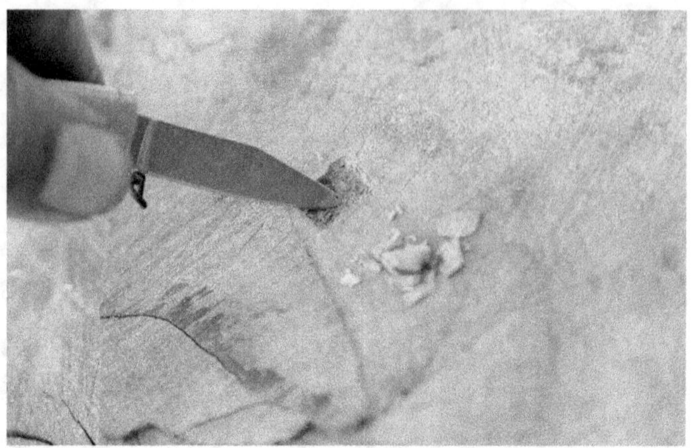

3. Use a knife or any sharp object to cut a small, V-shaped notch in the center of your fire board. Make sure that your notch is just big enough to hold your spindle stick.

4. Place small pieces of bark underneath the notch. The bark will be used to catch an ember from the friction between the spindle and fire board.

5. Take your spindle stick, which should be a thin stick about two feet long and half an inch in diameter, and place it in the V-shaped notch in the center of your fire board.

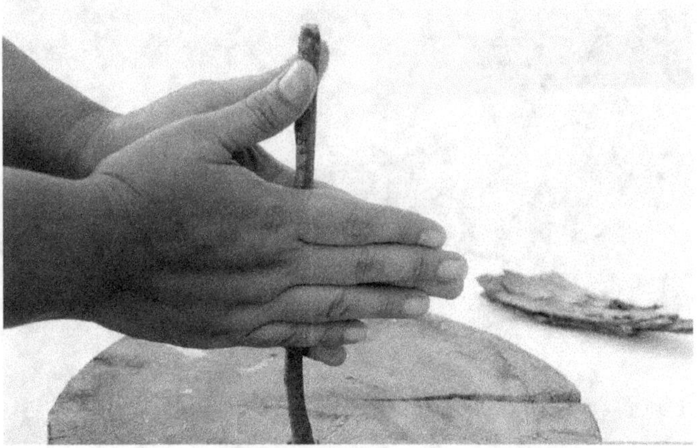

6. Hold the spindle stick between your two flat palms and begin to roll the spindle back and forth. Be sure to push the spindle stick firmly down into the fire board.

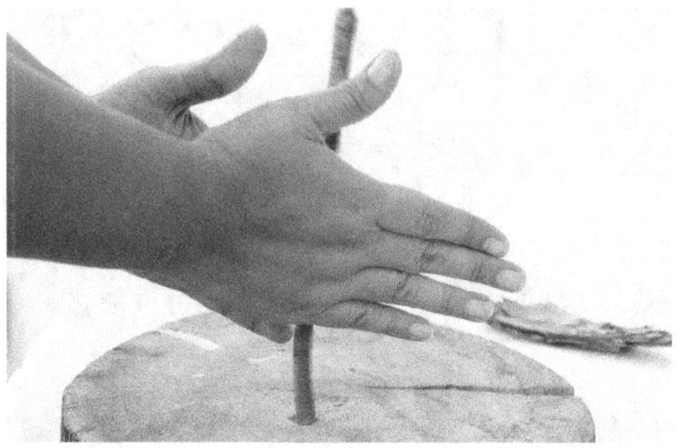

7. Continue to roll the spindle quickly between your hands, pushing one hand forward and then the other, until an ember is formed on the fire board.

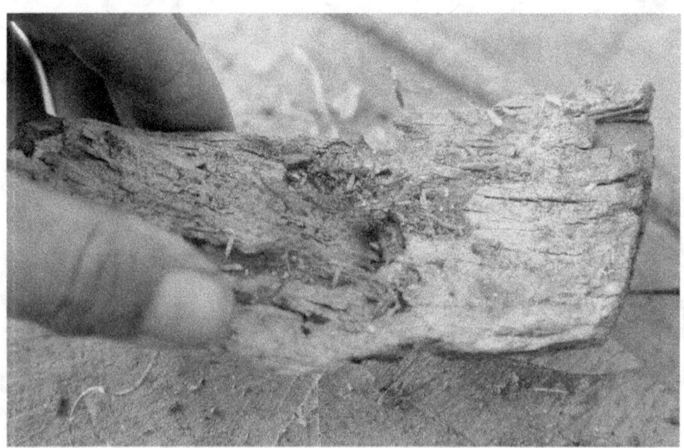

8. Transfer the glowing embers to a small piece of bark. You should have already placed a few small pieces of bark next to the notch for this purpose.

9. Place the bark containing the ember onto your tinder nest. Continue to blow gently on the tinder nest to fully transfer the ember and create a flame.

10. Begin to add increasingly larger pieces of wood to maintain a larger fire. Be advised that this method takes a while to create a fire, and requires physical as well as mental determination.

Method 6

Making a Bow Drill

1. Again, make a tinder nest. Use any dry plant material you can gather.

2. Find an object to use as a socket such as a stone or a heavy piece of wood. The socket will be used to put pressure on the spindle.

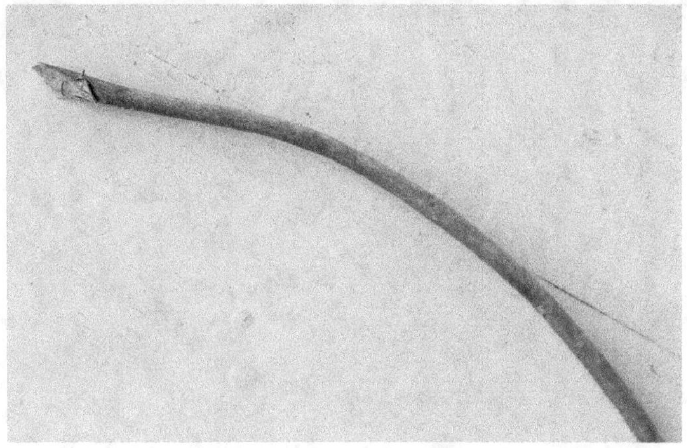

3. Find a long, flexible piece of wood about the length of your arm. It is best if this piece of wood has a slight curve in it. This will serve as the handle of your bow.

4. Make the string of the bow using any strong, abrasive material that can withstand a lot of friction. You might want to use a shoelace, a thin rope or string, paracord, or a strip of rawhide.

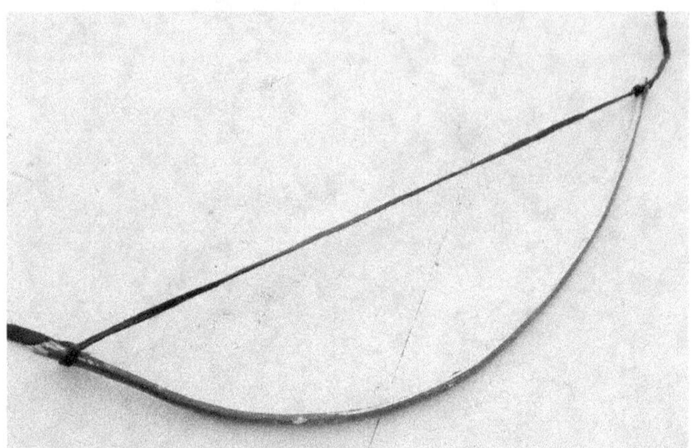

5. Tie the string as tight as possible to each end of the bow handle. If there are not already natural notches in the bow wood to anchor the string, whittle small, straight notches into the wood in order to act as a groove for the string.

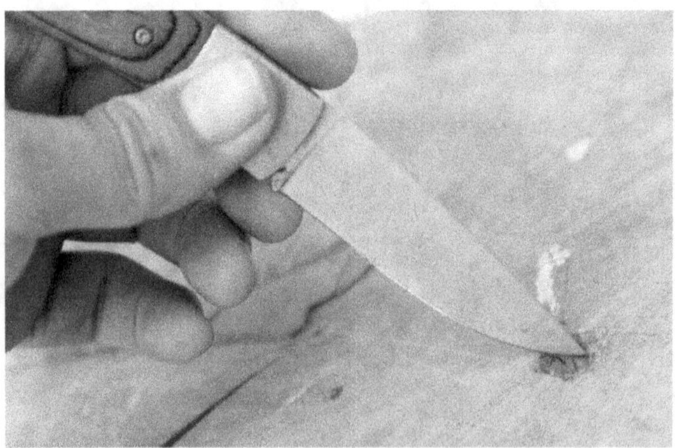

6. Find a piece of wood to use as the base of your hand drill, otherwise known as a fire board, and cut a small V-shaped notch into the center using a knife or other sharp object.

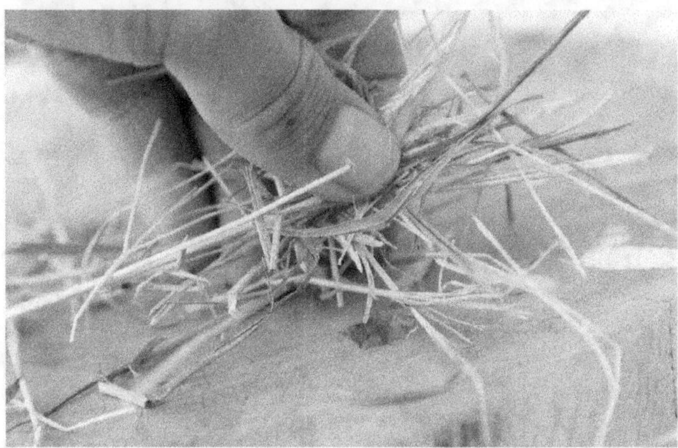

7. Place your tinder nest underneath the V-shaped notch. You want to have the tinder right next to base of the spindle so that you can easily create flames.

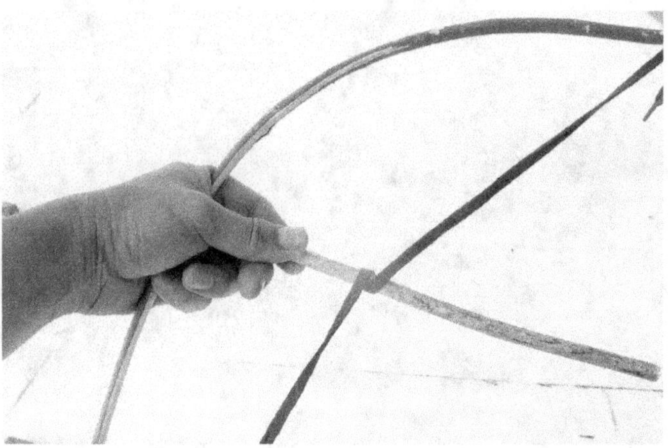

8. Loop the bow string around your spindle stick one time. Make sure you do so in the middle of the bow string to create enough space to roll the string back and forth.

9. Whittle one end of the spindle into a point, to reduce friction in the socket. Once a char starts on this end, avoid cutting it off to make the spindle last longer.

10. Place one end of the spindle in the V-shaped notch in your fire board and then stack the socket on the top end of the spindle. Hold the socket with your non-dominant hand.

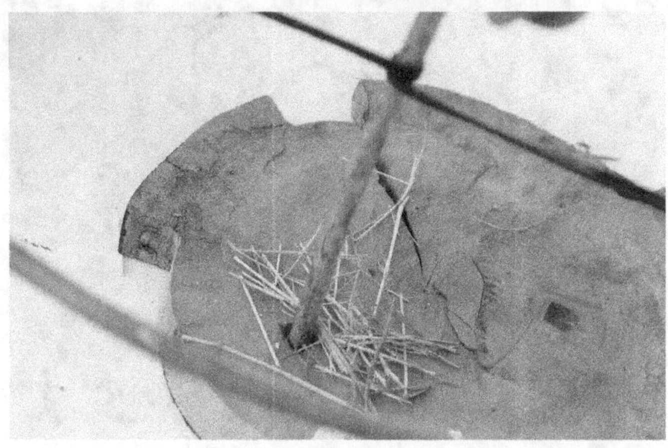

11. Begin sawing the bow quickly back and forth, holding the curved, wooden part of the bow in your dominant hand. This will cause the spindle to spin (hence the name "spindle") and create heat at the base of the fire board.

12. Continue to saw back and forth until you create an ember where the spindle meets the fire board. Make sure your tinder nest is close by.

13. Gather the ember you created onto a piece of scrap wood and drop it into your tinder nest. You may just be able to slide the ember off of the fire board into your tinder nest.

14. Blow on your tinder nest as you gradually add increasingly larger pieces of dry wood to create a fire.

Staying warm and dry as well as shielded from the elements of nature can revive your system, heal your body and relax your mind.

Fire will keep you refreshed and ready for the next step in surviving the harsh reality of the zombie apocalypse that waits outside your shelter.

The warmth and protection of fire is a great deterrent to wild animals such as bears, coyotes and other creatures that undoubtedly will also be in search for food and shelter too.

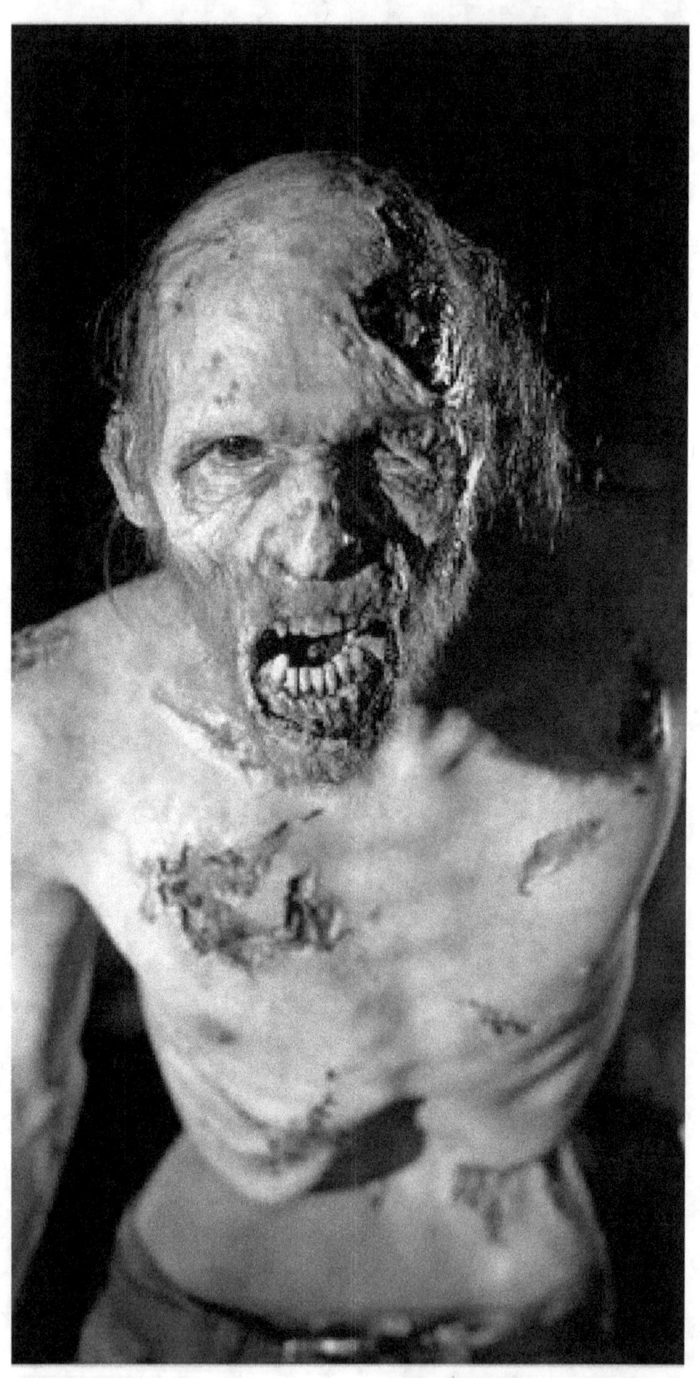

THE THIRST FOR LIFE

The most basic component to life sustenance is that of H2O, Water. The life giving liquid that replenishes the body. Without water the body quickly dehydrates and organs begin to stop functioning.

So, for all the preparation that you might do to survive the fallout of the raging zombie virus and the attacking hordes of flesh eating dead. If you do not have a source of water it will be mere days until your body shuts down and you pass out. Making all those preparations void.

Water

A human being can survive an average of three to five days without the intake of water. The issues presented by the need for water dictate that unnecessary water loss by perspiration be avoided in survival situations. The need for water increases with exercise.

A typical person will lose minimally two to maximally four liters of water per day under ordinary conditions, and more in hot, dry, or cold weather. Four to six liters of water or other liquids are generally required each day in the wilderness to avoid dehydration and to keep the body functioning properly. The U.S. Army survival manual does not recommend that you drink water only when thirsty, as this leads to under hydrating. Instead, water should be drunk at regular intervals. Other groups recommend rationing water through "water discipline".

A lack of water causes dehydration, which may result in lethargy, headaches, dizziness, confusion, and eventually death. Even mild dehydration reduces endurance and impairs concentration, which is dangerous in a survival situation where clear thinking is essential. Dark yellow or brown urine is a diagnostic indicator of dehydration. To avoid dehydration, a high priority is typically assigned to locating a supply of drinking water and making provision to render that water as safe as possible.

Recent thinking is that boiling or commercial filters are significantly safer than the use of chemicals, with the exception of chlorine dioxide.

When the water you're hoping to drink might be riddled with parasites or bacteria, you can't afford to skimp on water purification. In the very circumstances that put you in contact with questionable water (being in the wilderness, surviving or recovering from a disaster, or living in a part of the world where water isn't purified for you) the last thing you want to do is to get sick. Read the following instructions carefully to learn how to purify your own water.

Method 1
Filtering Water while Camping

1. Consider a physical filter. "Pump filters" may be your cheapest option in this category, but can be slow and tedious. For long trips, look into "gravity filters," which are typically a pair of bags connected by a hose. The bag with the filter is filled with water, then hung up to let the water drain through the filter into the clean bag. This is a fast, convenient option that doesn't require you to carry around a supply of disposable filters.

These filters do not protect against viruses, but they are effective against bacteria. Not all wilderness areas require protection against viruses, however, especially in the US. Check your regional disease control center or a tourist information center for more information on the risks in your region.

Method 2
Iodine

1. Learn about chemical disinfection. Tablets are slow but cheap, and are effective against most bacteria and viruses. Tablets come in two common types:

Iodine tablets should be left in the water for at least 30 minutes. They are sometimes sold with a companion tablet for hiding the iodine taste.

Pregnant women and people with thyroid conditions should not use this method, and no one should use it as their main source of water for more than a few weeks.

Chlorine dioxide tablets normally have a 30 minute wait time. Unlike iodine, they are effective in areas contaminated by the bacterium Cryptosporidium – but only if you wait 4 hours before drinking.

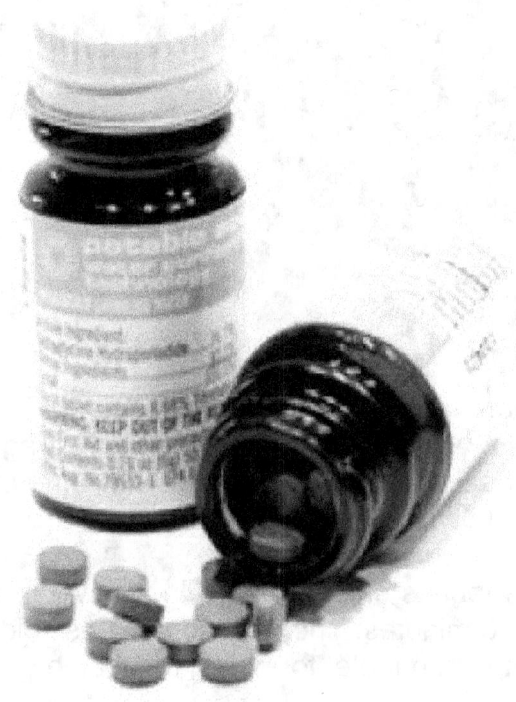

Method 3
Filtering Water while Camping

1. Boil water. This is an extremely effective method of killing pathogens, as long as you let the water boil for at least one minute. It may not be convenient to boil water several times a day, but be aware that you won't need additional filtration if you're already boiling water for your evening meal or morning coffee.

At high elevations, boil the water for at least three minutes, since the water will boil at a lower temperature in the thin air. The high temperature, not the boiling action itself, is responsible for killing bacteria and viruses.

Method 4
Filtering Water with Cloth

1. Drink straight from the spring source. If you're lucky enough to find a mountain spring bubbling from the rocks, it's usually safe to drink directly from it – but this does not apply even a couple feet (0.6 m) away.

This is not a foolproof rule, and may be dangerous in agricultural regions, areas with historic mining, or lower-elevation areas near population centers.

Method 5
Filtering Water with Charcoal

1. Make charcoal. Charcoal makes an excellent water filter, and is in fact the material used to filter water in many manufactured filters. You can make your own charcoal in the wild if you are able to build a fire. Built a hot wood fire and let it burn out completely. Cover it with dirt and ashes, and wait at least a few hours before digging it up again. Once it has completely cooled, break up the charred wood into tiny pieces, or even into dust. You've now created your own charcoal.

While not as effective as store-bought "activated charcoal," which is not feasible to produce in the wilderness, homemade charcoal should be plenty effective in a filter.

2. Tightly pack the charcoal over the cloth. Pack the charcoal dust and pieces as tightly as possible over the cloth. For the filter to be effective, all water must drip slowly through the charcoal. If the water runs easily through your filter, you'll need to try again and tightly pack more charcoal into it. You should end up with a thick, tightly packed layer – up to half the container's depth, if you are using a water bottle as your filter.

3. Cover the charcoal with pebbles, sand, and more cloth. If you can spare a second layer of cloth, cover the charcoal tightly to prevent is being stirred up when you pour water into the container. Whether or not you add the cloth, of small pebbles and/or sand are recommended to catch larger debris and keep the charcoal in place.

Grass and leaves can also be used, as long as you know they are not poisonous species.

Method 6
Cloth Filter

1. Use cloth to cover the top container's filtration hole. Stretch the fabric over the base of the top container. Use enough cloth to completely cover the base, or the charcoal could be washed through.

Method 7
Filtering Water With Tree Bark

1. Form a cone out of a strip of bark. Birch bark, or a bark similar to it, is best for creating this filtering system because it is flexible but will keep its shape. Keep in mind that this method will not fully purify the water, but it will reduce the number of microbes in the water. This method should only be used in extreme emergencies.

• If you are having a hard time keeping your bark in the shape of a cone, you could try tying a piece of rope or a durable type of grass around it to keep its shape.

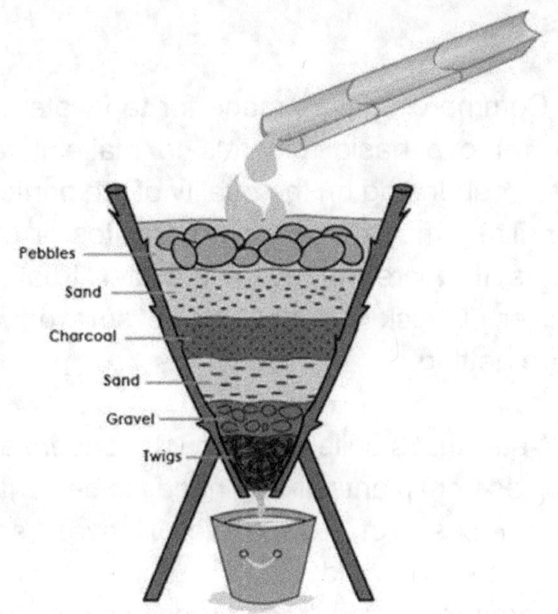

2. Layer the cone. Wildwood Survival suggests layering the cone with sand, charcoal, grass, and gravel (or small rocks.) Charcoal is especially good for removing bacteria. If you had a fire, crush up some of the burnt pieces of wood.

3. Pour the water through the cone and into a container. Do this several times to increase the amount of purification that occurs. Again, this method does not guarantee purification, but it will remove a good deal of the contaminants in the water.

Tips

• Commercial filters made for tap water may only remove basic minerals to make it taste better, depending on the quality of the particular filter. They may not remove parasites or other threats that are removed in water treatment facilities. Check the label to be sure of what you're getting.

• Water that's collected through condensation (such as from plants or soil) needs to be purified. The process of evaporation leaves some sediments behind, but unless boiling temperature is reached, parasites and other harmful substances may still be in the water.

• Both bleach and iodine work much better in warm water.

Warnings

• Chlorine and iodine can be toxic. Do not use more of either chemical than indicated, or use only in emergency situations.

• All the methods indicated above are designed to remove biological threats only, such as bacteria. They generally do not remove chemical (for example, industrial waste such as aluminum sludge) or radioactive contamination.

If it is suspected that the water contains such contaminants, rely on distillation, or weigh consumption against the risk of being dehydrated.

Use stainless steel water bottles. Plastic bottles are only designed to be filled and used once, since the plastic can break down over time, adding potentially harmful chemicals to the water and even harboring bacteria. Even aluminum bottles often have an inner plastic coating, and are not dishwasher safe, making them difficult to clean.

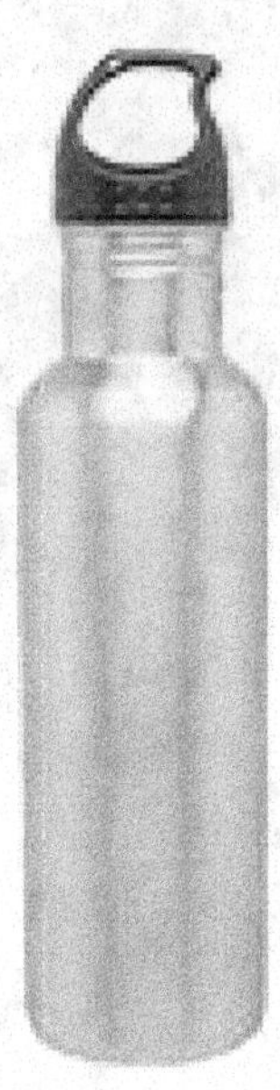

PLAY IT SAFE

When the walking dead appear on your doorstep, the next move will be yours. Knowing how to defend yourself and how to protect your family will be paramount.

More insight on safety

1. Malls as previously said are not a safe place to hide out, but they are cleared and sealed, you will have a large supply of items at your disposal. Entertainment wise, you can lay multiple games and watch many movies. You can even read. Weapon wise, it is hard to find a gun shop, but sports shops still provide numerous close-range weapons. Hardware stores also supply duct tape. A crucial piece of survival because you can combine items so you can get an even better tool of mass destruction (i.e. tape two knives to the end of a stick, and you got yourself a makeshift spear).

2. When it comes to traveling, you would want a sturdy vehicle which could take damage. Pick-ups, Jeeps, or Hummers are the ideal means of transportation. I especially like the idea of taking off a small part of the roof so someone can blast the heads off of the brain-eating infected while still being protected by the vehicle. Also, open the windows halfway so you can shoot from there.

3. The best number of people in a group are 4-5 people. Each person should pack up a nice supply of food, weapons, duct tape, and batteries. Once you find your safe house, try to stay for the night and find more supplies.

- Each member should be able to at least do one of the following:

- Sprint for at least five minutes.

- Carryover twenty pounds of gear.

- Know how to do first-aid.

- Know how to use any weapon.

- Be willing to contribute to the group.

Defending Yourself & Your Family

Disasters often bring out the best in people. Unfortunately they also brings out the worst. After any disaster, whether local or widespread, there will be individual's intent upon creating mischief. Lawlessness and disorder frequently become the rule of the day. While some individuals are lending their neighbors a helping hand, others will be helping themselves. There will be looting, stealing and an increase in acts of violence. Gang violence will become more common, even among individuals who formerly took no part in gangs. The police will be overwhelmed, so the responsibility will fall on the individual to provide protection for self and family.

Even a well-armed individual will be unable to hold out long if there is a violent gang intent upon taking his or her possessions. Your chances for survival will increase substantially if you are able to ban together with your neighbors for your mutual defense. In our cities these days it is unfortunate that neighbors can sometimes live side-by-side for years without getting to know each other. As we will see in the chapter dealing with the social aspects of survival, I recommend that you get to know your neighbors and befriend as many as you can. Don't wait until a disaster occurs. Do it now! Someday your life may depend on it.

After a disaster the police may have their hands full in more ways than one. History has shown that during any emergency there will be individuals in law enforcement who will abuse their authority. In the months following hurricane Katrina, 200 New Orleans police officers were disciplined for various offenses, including looting, which were committed during the chaos that enveloped the city after the hurricane.

Four police officers were indicted for first degree murder of unarmed individuals, including a 40-year-old retarded man who was shot five times in the back. Three other officers were charged with attempted murder. Two committed suicide.

I do not mean to imply that all police are bad. The vast majority are well-intentioned law abiding citizens who will risk their lives in order to protect others. But there are always individuals in the police force who will commit all sorts of crimes when the opportunity arises, and there is no better opportunity than when chaos is widespread. There will also be police officials who will think that they need and deserve your supplies more than you do, and will therefore commandeer them for their official or personal use. It will behoove you to lay low, keeping your activities and provisions a secret from the police. In fact, keeping your supplies a secret from everyone except your most immediate family is always a good idea.

These are a few of the most amusing questions ever asked on zombies. Here are a few.

Question;

What happens to all the flesh that the walkers eat?

Answer;

Well in an honest answer they defecate where ever they are standing. It is one main reason that the zombies wreak. You can smell an old zombie from really far away for obvious reasons.

Question;

Does eating infected flesh have an effect?

Answer;

Well yes. If you eat the infected flesh of a zombie you subsequently turn in to a zombie yourself. Just as if you were bitten by a zombie. Since zombies carry a virus you would essentially be infected by that same virus.

Question;

Do the walkers that get killed by a blow to the head reanimate again?

Answer;

Bodily trauma that would kill a normal human, including decapitation, dismemberment and severe burns are not enough to kill a zombie. The only thing shown to be effective in permanently stopping a zombie is significant damage to or destruction of the brain. A "blow to the head" would not kill a zombie at all, unless it was severe enough to damage whatever it is in the brain that keeps them animated. Once killed, zombies do not reanimate

Question;

Why do zombies eat our brains?

Answer;

There is an official explanation it is from a quote from Return of the Living Dead's writer and director, Dan O'Bannon, who suggested that the undead felt the need to feed on the brains of the recently living because it **somehow made them feel better** by easing their pain.

Question;

What are all the different names for zombies?

Answer:

This answer represents the best information I was able to find regarding the media -

1. BITERS
2. COLD BODIES
3. CREEPERS
4. DEAD ONES
5. FLOATERS/SWIMMERS
6. GEEKS
7. LAMEBRAINS
8. LURKERS
9. ROAMERS
10. MONSTERS
11. ROTTERS
12. SKIN EATERS
13. WALKERS.
14. STINKERS
15. SKIN BAGS
16. MEAT PUPPETS
17. EMPTIES
18. DEADIES
19. GHOULS
20. DEAD-HEADS
21. INFECTED
22. ZOMBIES

Question;

Where is the best place to hide if the zombies come?

Answer:

There are two types of hiding places: long-term and short-term.

Either way, a mall is the worst place to hide. Although it is probably loaded with supplies, it is impossible to clear (or will take a long time at least, the time you don't have). And then once you have cleared it, there is still the fact that there is how many entrances to cover. Not a good idea. For the short term, the following are good ideas:

A house can be ideal. Preferably an acreage. If it's perched on a hill, even better. The seclusion lowers the number of zombies and makes it harder for them to sneak up. It gives fewer entrances and should still hold a few basic survival items. Make sure you board up excess windows but if you have a room you don't be in a lot, maybe keep the window open for scouting.

Jam or block the doors, if there is only one, you picked a bad house. If the house has twenty entrances/exits, you picked a bad one as well. 2-4 is ideal because it gives you escape options, but few places the zombie can penetrate so easy to manage.

Long-term, as said above, is without a doubt an island. However, the zombie apocalypse motto is "If you can't beat them, don't join them" so do not become a zombie, please. Islands provide the best seclusion, and although it is not good for short-term once prepped, you can just live without interruption.

Intruder Alerts

If you have an intruder alarm in your home you will want to have a reliable battery back-up that will work even when the electricity is off for an extended period of time. If you do not have such a system a very effective yet inexpensive alternative is to install wireless, battery operated Sonic Alarms above each door and vulnerable window.

Sonic alarms are easily installed with the self-stick tape backing included on each unit. When the door is opened a magnetic switch activates the device which emits an ear-piercing sound that is sure to startle any intruder and awaken everyone in the house. Most intruders will immediately flee the scene when they hear such an alarm so you will probably never see them or have to confront them. If you do have to confront them it will be on your terms, with your weapon in hand, which is far better than being awakened in your bed with a gun at your head or a knife at your throat!

Ten top tips for fighting zombies!

1. Organize before they rise!

2. They feel no fear, why should you?

3. Use your head: cut off theirs.

4. Blades don't need reloading

5. Ideal protection: tight clothes, short hair.

6. Get up the staircase, then destroy it.

7. Get out of the car, get onto the bike.

8. Keep moving, keep low, keep quiet, and keep alert!

9. No place is safe, only safer.

10. The zombie may be gone, but the threat lives on.

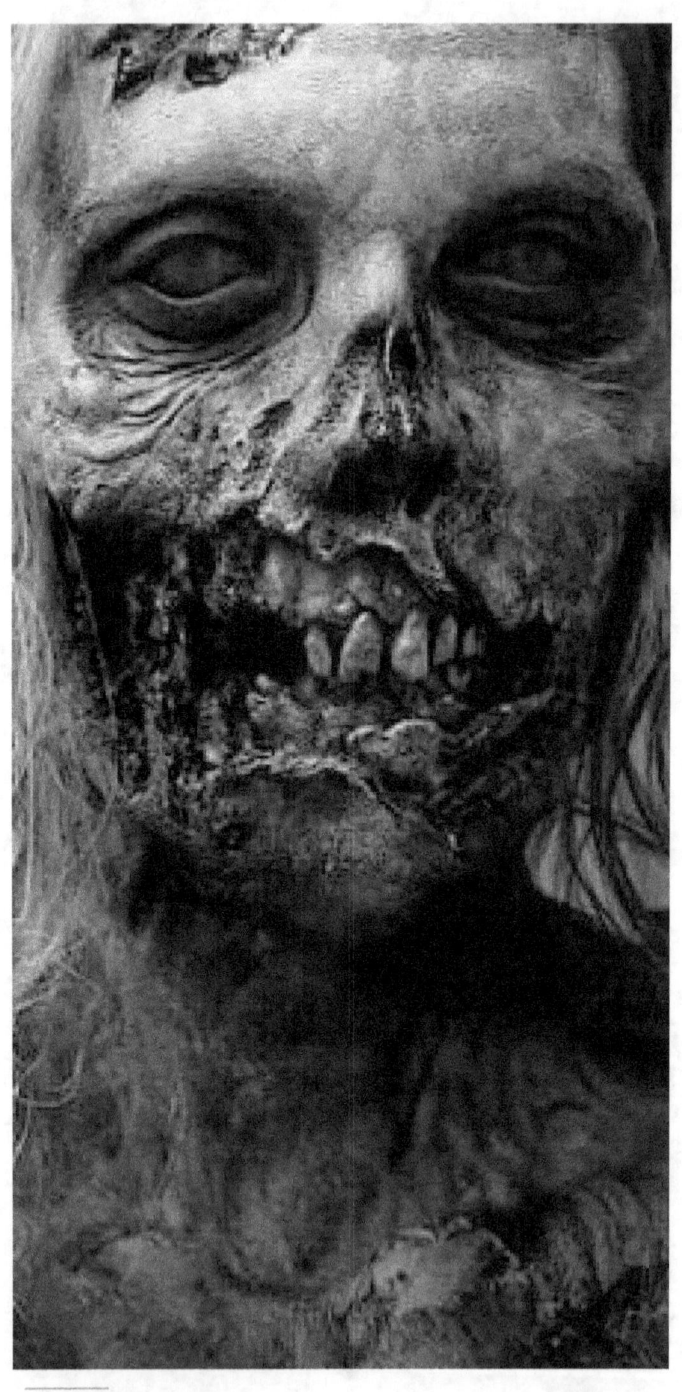

PUT YOUR SELF TO THE TEST

Once the zombie apocalypse begins you will have your work cut-out for you. Not only building shelters, administering first aid to those who need it, feeding your family and friends and fighting off the undead. All in a day's work maybe.

Understand the Risks in Your Neighborhood

The bad news is that natural disasters seem to be increasingly common, thanks to global warming. And TIME reports that this trend is even more troubling once you consider that coastal areas, which may suffer the most extreme disasters, are becoming ever more densely populated.

If you are considering moving to a new neighborhood, city or state, make sure you are comfortable with the natural risks associated with those areas. Neighborhoods in New York that were hit the hardest, like lower Manhattan, Battery Park, Red Hook, and Dumbo are very popular neighborhoods, in part because of their proximity to the water, but that also means your property will be more at risk if it's at or near sea level. Make sure you understand the risks attached to your neighborhood, be they low elevation, proximity to a fault line or nearness to a flood zone.

Have an Emergency Fund

Saving an emergency fund (at least six months of net pay) is important for many reasons like if you lose a job, your car breaks down or you have to pay off an unexpected medical cost. We know, sometimes having a rainy day fund seems like the least important thing to save for—but it's for times when more than a rainy day strikes (like this week) that make it necessary. Should you be affected by a natural disaster, it will protect you from sinking into debt should you be displaced from your home, need to replace items not covered by insurance or are unable to work due to the disaster.

During the zombie apocalypse, money will come in handy for buying goods or services. Especially when there will be food and water shortages and supply deficiencies as well. Do not think that your local friendly neighborhood grocery store or gas station will not inflate prices or price gauge when disaster strikes. During disasters there will always be those who attempt to benefit from it financially.

So be prepared to buy a gallon of milk for $20 or a gallon of gas for $100 or more. Depending on the severity of the areas affected. Use your money wisely.

Outrunning a zombie?

Things I fear the most: spiders, bees, and zombies. While I know how to deal with the first two threats, I must constantly study how to off a zombie before I become one. Yet, the hardest part of studying good tactics for a zombie war is that it hasn't happened yet; there is no comparison to base how one would destroy these creatures. The only thing we have to prepare ourselves for a possible zombie attack is sound logic. That's when it becomes necessary to debunk the myths that many horror movies show, however, make no sense when you are really thrust into a world of zombies and survival. So here are the most basic myths that should be dismissed:

So the question I sthis, Can you outrun a zombie? Well, no and yes. Unlike the movies, when a zombie is first turned they undergo a stage when their bodies physically die.

Immediately after the death occurs the zombie suffers rigor mortis (a stiffening of joints and muscles) for the first few days until the muscles eventually return to a permanently altered state. The ability to run down or slowly slide to a living person depends on the state of the zombie before they were changed.

If a person was a runner before being changed then they will most likely be a good runner in the post-apocalyptic theory, if not better. The reason I say that zombie might now be a better runner is that muscle fatigue will no longer affect the body. Therefore, the ability to feel no pain will keep the zombie running until the living person it is after is devoured, or the human he is chasing moves from the sensory range of the zombie.

Yet, the chances of meeting a sprinting zombie are as slim as meeting a triathlon neighbor in today's society. Luckily, this is the rare moment when I would actually thank America for being out of shape. Yet, the flip side of this is that based on America's low health scores many of us wouldn't even be able to out-walk a zombie without overly frequent rest stops or a double Mocha frap chino expresso from the local coffee shop.

THE BASIC SURVIVAL GUIDE FOR THE ZOMBIE APOCALYPSE

Would you survive the Zombie Apocalypse, and lead your friends and family to safety?

If zombies came would you just coward down and cry? Or will you man up and become a hero! And kill some zombies?

This quiz will let you know by asking your personal questions and what would you do situations.

1) How old are you?
   A. 10-14
   B. 15-19
   C. 20-25
   D. 30-40
   E. 41-45
   F. 46+

2) How much do you exercise weekly?
   None
   A. 1-2 hours a week
   B. 3-4 hours a week
   C. 5-6 hours a week
   D. 7+ hours a week

3) Your hobbies?

   A. Playing on the computer.

   B. Watching TV, playing video games.

   C. Sports

   D. Drinking, smoking and partying

   E. Fighting

   F. Sports, playing games, watching tv.

   G. Hunting

4) How familiar are you with zombies?

   A. Very! I love zombies, I dream about them coming.

   B. A little I guess, shoot them in the head right?

   C. None, zombies are pretty stupid...

   D. Well, they burn easily.

   E. I played 1 or 2 games I guess I okay with them.

5)   How would you first react to hearing that zombies are attacking, and will be to your city in a few hours?

A. Hell Yeah!! Grab my gun and do some killing.

B. I would be scared. Probably just hide in my corner and hope they don't find me.

C. Well first I'm kinda sad because I know some of my friends and family will die, but I will not let my emotions take over.

D. I would go get as many supplies (food, ammo, guns) as I could and start barricading.

E. I would steal a fast vehicle, stay mobile.

7)   You are sitting at home with your family watching TV, when suddenly your program is interrupted by breaking news: the Zombie Apocalypse has begun. What do you do first?

    A. Ignore the outbreak; it's probably nothing.

    B. Google the outbreak; I need more information.

    C. Run outside screaming.

    D. Switch channels to American Idol.

8)   Your first thought is getting food, what do you get?

    A. Candy, it will keep me awake.

    B. Meat, I need my protein for killing.

    C. Canned food, it will last longer.

8) What kind of beverages?

A. All kinds, you need to have a variety

B. Alcohol, I am depressed everyone is dead

C. Energy drinks, coffee mixes, I need to stay awake

D. Water, it won't spoil so it's good for me.

9) You find a gun shop with a few guns for you and your buddies, what's your weapon of choice? (Guns)

A. Spaz-12 shotgun

B. M4 assault rifle, fully auto

C. M-21 sniper rifle

D. Desert Eagle

E. 9mm pistol

F. M1 Garand, semi-auto

10) Now you get to choose one melee weapon.

   A. Katana

   B. Machete

   C. Baseball bat

   D. Mace

   E. Hammer

   F. Bowie Knife

   G. Pocket Knife

   H. Iron Pipe

11) You come across a huge car lot with a very wide selection of vehicles, your vehicle of choice would be?

   A. Porsche, all you need is speed and handling baby

   B. Ford F-350, build that sucker up, it'll go through any zombie attack.

   C. Workers van, slow but will carry many people and supplies.

   D. Motorcycle, small quick very easy to get around.

12)   If you could choose between these places, where would you choose?

    A. Police station, weapons, some food,

    B. School, many rooms few doors, cafeteria food.

    C. Island, no one around and food, food, food.

    D. 2 story house.

    E. I won't be in just one place, staying mobile is the best idea.

13)   You and one of your buddy are surrounded by a group of about 20 zombies, you see you have 14 shells left with your gun, and you buddy has 2. Are you Dead?

    A. Basically, I will kill 14 of them and my buddy will save the last two for us.

    B. No, I will shoot a few and go thru a gap of them. And sprint for my life

    C. I will shoot as many as I can, then kill the rest with our melee weapons.

    D. Doesn't matter ill kill myself might as well do that instead of dying by zombies, and let some wanderer get some weapons.

13)   Your best friend or Bf/Gf has been bitten, what do you do?

A. Kill them in a heartbeat

B. Say sorry and goodbye, live the last seconds with them and tell them how great they were, then kill them before they turn.

C. Just let them go, and run away

D. Keep them forever and ever. Tie them up and wait till they turn, and walk with a lasso with a pole on it.

14)   You see someone getting chased by 4 zombies, while you're looking for food. What do you do?

A. Stay hidden indoors, hoping he doesn't run in there with you

B. Run out there and help him.

C. Throw a weapon out the door and hide inside, hoping he saw it. But doesn't run in.

15)   You're in a two-story apartment building upstairs. How do you protect yourself?

A. Barricade the stairs doors and windows, zombies are not that strong.

B. Don't do anything to it, they can't smell you, so why bring more attention than needed?

C. Destroy the stairs and put a rope ladder at the top.

16)   If you're in the middle of town and you see a group of zombies coming from the north, what do you do?

A. Run 3 in a half miles east to your house.

B. Run 4 miles west to the school.

C. Run 1 mile east and 5 miles north to a mall, just to get around them.

D. Run 15 miles south to a military fort that you were going to. Hopefully, zombies get tired too.

17)   Okay, some of the basic questions.
How do you kill zombies?

    A. By shooting your whole clip...Duh

    B. Destroying the brain.

    C. Shoot their legs off and watch them crawl until the bleed to death....or whatever they do.

    D. Jab their eyeballs out

    E. Cut their wrists

18)   Can zombies climb?

    A. Yes

    B. No

19)   Will you be prepared for zombies if they do happen?

    A. No, it will never happen

    B. Well I'll be as ready as I'll ever be, who knows if they'll come

    C. Yes, I already built a bunker.

20) You've verified that the Zombie Apocalypse is for real. It's happening right NOW! You have no time to waste! What is your top priority?

    A. Rescuing my loved ones.

    B. Barricading my house. Safety first.

    C. Creating makeshift explosives.

    D. Run outside screaming.

21) Now that you're safe, you must come up with a long-term plan. How will you and your family deal with the outbreak?

    A. Hunker down in our house.

    B. Bolt for the countryside.

    C. Load up all useful supplies, and prepare to leave.

    D. Loot our neighbors; now's the time for riches!

22)   A family member is bitten in the attempt to escape. What do you do?

  A. Leave him/her behind.
  B. Cut off the infected limb.
  C. Shoot him/her immediately.
  D. Bandage the wound and keep a careful eye on him/her. Maybe we can learn something?

23)   You reach a small town, where there is no sign of the Infected. In fact, nobody in the town even knows about the Zombie Apocalypse. What do you do?

  A. Gun in with guns blazing; we can take over the town!
  B. Immediately take the opportunity to get rid of our useless cash for valuable supplies.
  C. Donate supplies to the villages in good will.
  D. Onwards!

24)   The world has fallen; the Zombies have won. You're backed into a corner, and have nowhere left to run.

A. Push family members into zombies to buy you time to run.

B. Shoot myself.

C. Charge into the zombies, taking as many of them down as you can.

D. Never give up; rapidly search for escape route.

25)   You've lost friends and family on your journey, but for now you've escaped the immediate peril of the Apocalypse. You managed to get to a sail boat on a lake. One day you see a group of survivors at the docks. They're fighting off zombies, and it looks like they won't last much longer.

A. Immediately try to rescue them. What is the point of life, if not to help each other?

B. Sadly observe from a distance, as they die one by one.

C. Turn up the music; life goes on.

D. Resume fishing.

26)   Over the next few years you have grown wise and experienced, and have adapted to the new world. You now lead a band of survivors, and they look to you for leadership. Your group is probably humanity's last hope. What is your goal?

A. To kill as many zombies as possible.

B. To rescue as many survivors as possible.

C. To begin rebuilding a city, where we can be safe. Slowly reclaim the country.

D. Survival is the only goal.

27)   You have a Motorcycle. 5 Survivors are asking for escape. Bearing that none of the people have equipment, who do you take?
An Unknown Man wearing my countries Military Uniform

A. A vaguely recognizable Police Officer

B. A family member

C. Your best friend

D. A beautiful member of the opposite or preferred Sex

E. None, I have more room for supplies then

28) You rebuild and develop somewhere safe and reliable to live. Your group is growing crops, and working to fortify and better the city. You are about to retire as leader of your people; What knowledge do you wish to impart to the young children growing up in this world?

A. Survival!

B. Always be suspicious.

C. Trust! We will eventually fail if we can't trust each other.

D. Weapons! Learn how to fight, and learn how to kill.

29) How do you plan to survive long term?

A. Raiding for supplies

B. Securing a Fort and farming

C. I haven't thought that far ahead

D. I'm focusing on short term

E. I don't think I'll live that long

30) Last Question. Theoretical. You're starving, yet you and your armed troops know where a lightly defended survivor camp is. The survivor camp is not willing to share food with you. What do you do?

E. Compassion! Never kill a zombie unless absolutely necessary. Zombies were once like us.

F. Flee the city and let the raiders take it. Better that than more lives being lost.

G. Continue to defend the city, slowly losing men to guerrilla warfare tactics.

H. Deceive the enemy into thinking we surrender, and then kill all who come. Life is tough. We must survive!

I. Venture out of the city, and attack the raiders!

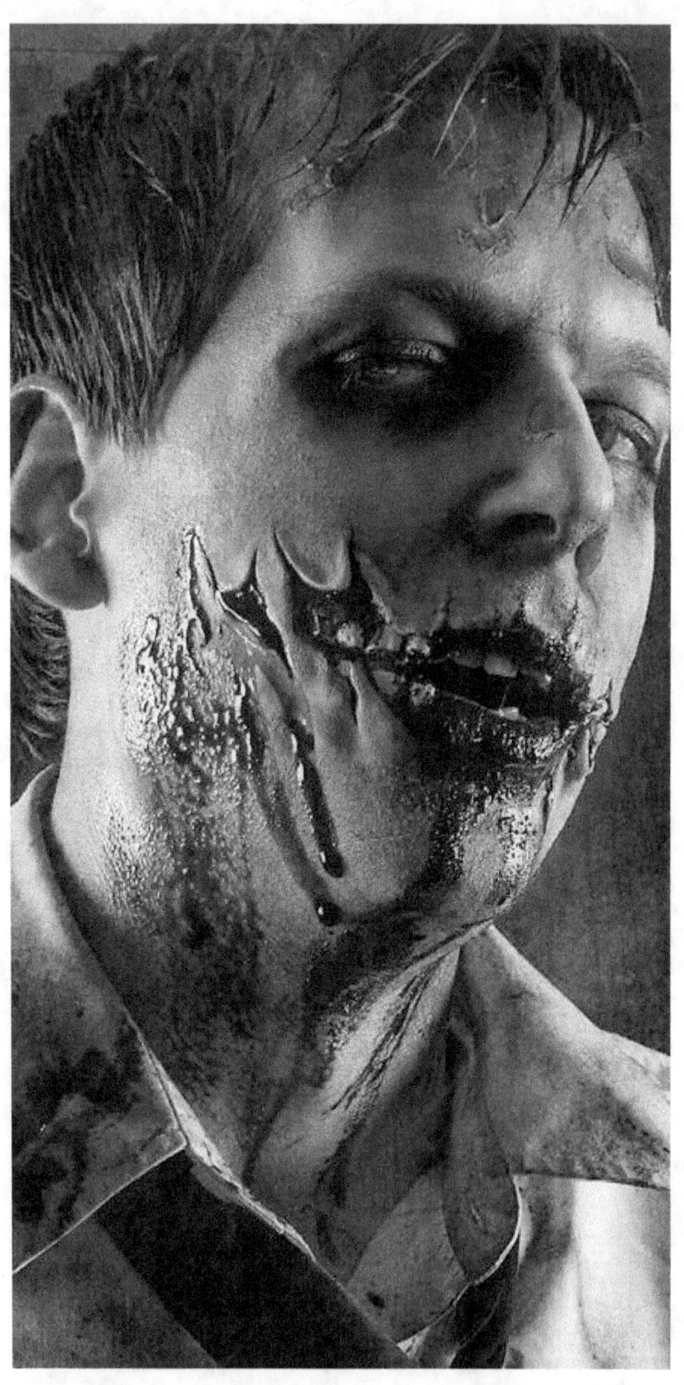

THE END IS NEAR

So now that you know what to do, you now understand the importance of disaster preparedness and safety.

Knowing is half the battle when it comes to dealing with disasters, whether it is a force of nature, or alien spacecraft attacking the earth.

Having the appropriate knowledge to not only survive but to thrive in a chaotic world overrun by the flesh-eating decaying dead, is what will make the difference. Separating yourself and your family from those who will be eaten and devoured by the walking dead like a hot dog eating contest will ensure your survival and help you deal with the hordes of zombies in the apocalyptic future.

As you ultimately make your way through the decaying world around you, you will have the firm knowledge and skills to better understand your place in it. Once you have settled into your environment and become self-sustaining, you will have the foresight to recognize the perils and pitfalls that await you in this post-calamity era. Knowing where to go and where not to go, to build your own shelter, to starting your own fire and feeding your family and extended circle as well.

According to a 2009 Carleton University and University of Ottawa epidemiological analysis, an outbreak of even *Living Dead*'s slow zombies "is likely to lead to the collapse of civilization, unless it is dealt with quickly."

Based on their mathematical modelling, the authors concluded that offensive strategies were much more reliable than quarantine strategies, due to various risks that can compromise a quarantine. They also found that discovering a cure would merely leave few humans alive, since this would do little to slow the infection rate.

On a longer time scale, the researchers noted that all humans would eventually end up turned or dead. This is because the main epidemiological risk of zombies, besides the difficulties of neutralizing them, is that their population just keeps increasing; generations of humans merely "surviving" still have a tendency to feed zombie populations, resulting in gross outnumbering. The researchers explain that their methods of modelling may be applicable to the spread of political views or diseases with dormant infection.

The Zombie Institute for Theoretical Studies (ZITS) is a program through the University of Glasgow. The ZITS team is dedicated to using real science to explain what could be expected in the event of an actual zombie apocalypse. Much of their research is used to disprove common beliefs about the zombie apocalypse as shown in popular media. They have published one book (Zombie Science 1Z) and give public "spoof" lectures on the subject.

Philosopher Nick Bostrom classifies risks according to their scope and intensity. A "global catastrophic risk" is any risk that is at least "global" in scope, and is not subjectively "imperceptible" in intensity. Those that are at least "trans-generational" (affecting all future generations) in scope and "terminal" in intensity are classified as existential risks. While a global catastrophic risk may kill the vast majority of life on earth, humanity could still potentially recover. An existential risk, on the other hand, is one that either destroys humanity (and, presumably, all but the most rudimentary species of non-human lifeforms and/or plant life) entirely or at least prevents any chance of civilization recovering. Bostrom considers existential risks to be far more significant.

Similarly, in *Catastrophe: Risk and Response*, Richard Posner singles out and groups together events that bring about "utter overthrow or ruin" on a global, rather than a "local or regional" scale. Posner singles out such events as worthy of special attention on cost-benefit grounds because they could directly or indirectly jeopardize the survival of the human race as a whole. Posner's events include meteor impacts, runaway global warming, grey goo, bioterrorism, and particle accelerator accidents.

Researchers experience difficulty in studying near human extinction directly, since humanity has never been destroyed before in recorded history. While this does not mean that it will not be in the future, it does make modelling existential risks difficult, due in part to survivorship bias.

Dr. Bostrom identifies four types of existential risk. "Bangs" are sudden catastrophes, which may be accidental or deliberate. He thinks the most likely sources of bangs are malicious use of nanotechnology, nuclear war, and the possibility that the universe is a simulation that will end. "Crunches" are scenarios in which humanity survives but civilization is slowly destroyed. The most likely causes of this, he believes, are exhaustion of natural resources, a stable global government that prevents technological progress, or dysgenic pressures that lower average intelligence. "Shrieks" are undesirable futures. For example, if a single mind enhances its powers by merging with a computer, it could dominate human civilization. Bostrom believes that this scenario is most likely, followed by flawed superintelligence and a repressive totalitarian regime. "Whimpers" are the gradual decline of human civilization or current values. He thinks the most likely cause would be evolution changing moral preference, followed by extraterrestrial invasion.

Some risks, such as that from asteroid impact, with a one-in-a-million chance of causing humanity's extinction in the next century, have had their probabilities predicted using straightforward, well-understood, and (in principle) precise methods (although even in cases like these, the exact rate of large impacts is contested). Similarly, the frequency of volcanic eruptions of sufficient magnitude to cause catastrophic climate change, similar to the Toba Eruption, which may have almost caused the extinction of the human race, has been estimated at about 1 in every 50,000 years.

The relative danger posed by other threats is much more difficult to calculate. Given the limitations of ordinary calculation and modeling, expert elicitation is frequently used instead to obtain probability estimates. In 2008, an informal survey of experts on different global catastrophic risks at the Global Catastrophic Risk Conference at the University of Oxford suggested a 19% chance of human extinction will happen by the year 2100.

The 2016 annual report by the Global Challenges Foundation estimates that an average American is more than five times more likely to die during a human-extinction event than in a car crash.

There are significant methodological challenges in estimating these risks with precision. Most attention has been given to risks to human civilization over the next 100 years, but forecasting for this length of time is difficult.

The types of threats posed by nature may prove relatively constant, though new risks could be discovered. Anthropogenic threats, however, are likely to change dramatically with the development of new technology; while volcanoes have been a threat throughout history, nuclear weapons have only been an issue since the 20th century.

Historically, the ability of experts to predict the future over these timescales has proved very limited. Man-made threats such as nuclear war or nanotechnology are harder to predict than natural threats, due to the inherent methodological difficulties in the social sciences. In general, it is hard to estimate the magnitude of the risk from this or other dangers, especially as both international relations and technology can change rapidly.

Existential risks pose unique challenges to prediction, even more than other long-term events, because of observation selection effects. Unlike with most events, the failure of a complete extinction event to occur in the past is not evidence against their likelihood in the future, because every world that has experienced such an extinction event has no observers, so regardless of their frequency, no civilization observes existential risks in its history. These anthropic issues can be avoided by looking at evidence that does not have such selection effects, such as asteroid impact craters on the Moon, or directly evaluating the likely impact of new technology.

In addition to known and tangible risks, unforeseeable viral or biological (Zombies) extinction events may occur, presenting an additional methodological problem.

Biotechnology can pose a global catastrophic risk in the form of bioengineered organisms (viruses, bacteria, fungi, plants or animals). In many cases the organism will be a pathogen of humans, livestock, crops or other organisms we depend upon (e.g. pollinators or gut bacteria). However, any organism able to catastrophically disrupt ecosystem functions, e.g. highly competitive weeds, outcompeting essential crops, poses a biotechnology risk.

A biotechnology catastrophe may be caused by accidentally releasing a genetically engineered organism escaping from controlled environments, by the planned release of such an organism which then turns out to have unforeseen and catastrophic interactions with essential natural or agro-ecosystems, or by intentional usage of biological agents in biological warfare, bioterrorism attacks. Pathogens may be intentionally or unintentionally genetically modified to change virulence and other characteristics. For example, a group of Australian researchers unintentionally changed characteristics of the mouse pox virus while trying to develop a virus to sterilize rodents. The modified virus became highly lethal even in vaccinated and naturally resistant mice. The technological means to genetically modify virus characteristics are likely to become more widely available in the future if not properly regulated.

Terrorist applications of biotechnology have historically been infrequent. To what extent this is due to a lack of capabilities or motivation is not resolved. However, given current development, more risk from novel, engineered pathogens is to be expected in the future.

Exponential growth has been observed in the biotechnology sector, and some organizations predict that this will lead to major increases in biotechnological capabilities in the coming decades. They argue that risks from biological warfare and bioterrorism are distinct from nuclear and chemical threats because biological pathogens are easier to mass-produce and their production is hard to control (especially as the technological capabilities are becoming available even to individual users).

A survey by the Future of Humanity Institute estimated a 2% probability of extinction from engineered pandemics by 2100. Several health organizations propose three categories of measures to reduce risks from biotechnology and natural pandemics: Regulation or prevention of potentially dangerous research, improved recognition of outbreaks and developing facilities to mitigate disease outbreaks (e.g. better and/or more widely distributed vaccines).

These reports and others do not confront the possibility that a terrorist group or person could manage such a virulent outbreak to destabilize or collapse a given society or governmental system. In doing so what would these outbreaks look like? What ramifications do they bring beyond their intended purposes? Even in its basic form the drug Pyrrolidinopentiophenone or "Flakka" , produces a state in humans that make the user feel veracious hunger that can only be quenched by feeding on other human flesh. A scary side effect for sure. Since it is a synthetic drug itself, there is no reasonable discouragement that other synthetic drugs made or strains of viral infections that have been modified by governmental organizations cannot mimic those same effects.

Remember that the Ebola outbreak in early 2014 started a result of a single patient. The Ebola outbreak that began in West Africa in early 2014 is the worst outbreak of this virus in history. The Ebola virus had a high mortality rate: in the three countries most affected by the outbreak — Guinea, Sierra Leone and Liberia — about 70 percent of the infected people died.

When Ebola virus came for the first time to a small village in Guinea, the victim was a toddler, who later became known to the world as Patient Zero. He died on Dec. 6, 2013, at age 2, and the domino effect of his illness has spiraled into the outbreak currently ravaging three nations in West Africa. Emile Ouamouno. Emile's 3-year-old sister, his mother and his grandmother all died by January.

The disease detectives who traced the Ebola outbreak back to the toddler still don't know how he got infected. The child may have contracted the disease through contact with a fruit bat, as the animals are reservoirs of the virus. Most likely, the outbreak started from only this toddler and no one else, the researchers said, because their genetic analysis of the viruses found in multiple patients' blood samples showed great similarities within the samples. This suggests that the outbreak started from a single introduction of the virus from animals into the human population, the researchers wrote in their report.

For those still in doubt that a viral infection might spread globally and infect humans with a deadly disease one should only look at the raw data for the pandemic Avian Flu in the late 1990's.

21 May 1997

Bird flu virus H5N1 is isolated for the first time from a human patient in Hong Kong. The virus infects 18 patients after close contact with poultry, with six deaths. Fortunately the virus does not spread from person to person. Within three days, Hong Kong's entire chicken population is slaughtered to prevent further outbreak.

Feb 2003

Alarm bells are again raised when the avian virus H5N1 infects two people in Hong Kong, one fatal.

28 Feb 2003

Outbreaks of chicken flu occur in The Netherlands due to the H7N7 avian flu virus. By April the virus has spread to nearly 800 poultry farms and resulted in the culling of almost 11 million chickens. The virus infects 83 people causing conjunctivitis and flu-like symptoms, and kills one man.

Dec 2003

South Korea has its first outbreak of avian flu in chickens, caused by H5N1.

Jan 2004

Japan has the first outbreak of avian influenza (H5N1) since 1925.
Jan 2004

WHO confirms H5N1 infection in 11 people, eight fatal, in Thailand and Vietnam, but no cases of person to person transmission. The virus has wreaked havoc among poultry in Thailand, Vietnam, Japan and South Korea, and has also appeared in a duck farm in China.

WHO is developing vaccine candidates using H5N1 viruses isolated in 2003 and 2004, at laboratories in the U.S. and U.K.

March 2004

Avian H5N1 flu virus becomes more widespread among bird flocks in Asia, and has caused 34 human cases, with 23 deaths.

6 April 2004

Avian influenza virus H7N3 confirmed in two poultry workers in British Columbia who developed flu-like symptoms.

July 2004

Several countries, including Thailand, Vietnam, China and Indonesia, report new infections in poultry with H5N1.

Aug 2004

H5N1 is reported to have killed an additional three people in Vietnam. Chinese scientists report H5N1 avian flu infection in pigs, raising concerns that the virus could exchange genes with human flu strains in this 'mixing vessel'.

H5N1 virus has spread throughout most of SE Asia, resulting in the culling of over 100 million chickens. In Vietnam and Thailand, the virus has infected at least 37 people, with 26 deaths.

Nov 2004

WHO warns that the H5N1 bird flu virus might spark a flu pandemic that could kill millions of people, and is concerned that "much of the world is unprepared for a pandemic" and needs to enhance preparedness to reduce its potential impact.

WHO officials meet with vaccine makers, public-health experts and government representatives in a bid to speed up the production of flu vaccines to avert a global pandemic.

Dec 2004

WHO reports the first human case of H5N1 in Vietnam since early September. Since the beginning of 2004, bird flu has caused the deaths of 32 people in Vietnam and Thailand, and millions of chickens across Asia.

Jan/Feb 2005

13 additional cases of bird flu have occurred in Vietnam since December 2004, 12 fatal.

Feb 2005

First report of a bird flu case from Cambodia. A report of probable person to person transmission of bird flu in Vietnam is published.

April 2005

Vietnam has reported a total of 60 laboratory confirmed human cases of H5N1 avian influenza since the outbreaks began, with 35 deaths; Thailand has confirmed a total of 17 infections of which 12 have been fatal, while Cambodia has confirmed two fatal cases.

May 2005

Rumors of human deaths in China from H5N1 remain unconfirmed, while the virus has killed more than 1000 migratory birds. Indonesia's government confirms reports of H5N1 infection in pigs.

19 May 2005

WHO reports 97 cases and 53 deaths from bird flu in Vietnam, Cambodia and Thailand since January 2004.

June 2005

Indonesia confirms a man exposed to sick chickens has been infected with a deadly strain of avian flu virus. The farm laborer shows no symptoms, but his blood carries antibodies to the H5N1 strain.

Bird flu becomes resistant to the low-cost amantadine family of antiviral drugs. Chinese farmers' use of the compound in chickens is blamed, a claim formally denied by Chinese authorities who pledge to investigate the claim.

The Philippines, so far the only Asian country unaffected by bird flu, report their first case in a town north of the capital, Manila, but do not confirm whether it is the H5N1 strain.

On 29 July, the World Health Organisation confirms that samples from an 8-year-old girl who died on the 14 July, two days after the death of her father, who was Indonesia's first confirmed human infection of influenza A (H5N1).

August 2005

The World Health Organization (WHO) confirms three new cases of H5N1 in Vietnam. Of the three individuals infected, two died. Since mid-December 2004, 20 of the 63 cases of H5N1 in Vietnam have been fatal.

Vaccine manufacturer Maine Biological Labs is fined $500,000 for smuggling a chicken flu virus into the US. In 1998 the Maine biotechnology company illegally imported the virus from Saudi Arabia so that it could develop a vaccine for a disease-plagued poultry farm in that country. The company then used falsified documents to send 8000 bottles of the newly-created vaccine back to Saudi Arabia.

Both Russia and Kazakhstan report outbreaks of avian influenza in poultry in late July that are confirmed H5N1 in early August. Outbreaks in both countries were attributed to contact between domestic birds and wild waterfowl via shared water sources.

In early August, an outbreak of H5N1 in poultry was detected in Tibet. Mongolia then issues an emergency report following the death of 89 migratory birds at two lakes in the northern part of the country.

September 2005

Three more laboratory-confirmed cases of H5N1 strike Indonesia. A 37-year-old woman dies on 10th September and is the fourth fatality associated with H5N1 to hit the country. Indonesia's third laboratory-confirmed case of H5N1 since July 2005 involves an 8-year-old boy who survives. Later, a 27-year-old woman from Jakarta, who developed symptoms after direct contact with diseased and dying chickens in her household, dies on 26 September.

The Lancet publishes an article on 12 August 2005 saying the flu drug Relenza is at least as effective as Tamiflu, but has fewer side effects and there is no evidence of resistance to Relenza, compared with resistance levels of up to 18% in those taking Tamiflu. The researchers recommend stockpiling both drugs.

Viet Nam officials retrospectively confirm an additional fatal case of H5N1 infection, bringing the total in Viet Nam since mid-December 2004 to 64 cases, a third of which (21) were fatalities.

Two independent studies, each reaching different conclusions, suggest it would be possible to contain an emerging pandemic if the virus was detected quickly, if it did not spread too fast, if sufficient antiviral drugs were deployed around the outbreak's epicenter, and if strict quarantine and other measures were also used employed.

President George W. Bush calls for an international partnership that would require countries facing an influenza outbreak to share information and samples with the WHO. But experts say research would speed up if the US Centers for Disease Control and Prevention's (CDC) influenza branch threw open its databases of virus sequences and immunological and epidemiological data, and complain that too few of the flu data collected by the CDC are made generally available.

October 2005

Greece becomes the first EU country with a bird flu infection as the country's Centre for Veterinary Institutes detects bird flu in one turkey on the eastern Aegean island of Chios. Officials confirm the virus is a member of the H5 strain, but not yet identified as H5N1.

On 13 October WHO states that tests conducted by the World Organization for Animal Health (OIE) confirm the presence of H5N1 avian influenza in samples taken from domestic birds in Turkey. Days later, the presence of the virus is confirmed in Romania.

A fifth laboratory-confirmed case of H5N1 is reported from Indonesia on 10 October 2005. The 21-year old Sumatran man had contact with diseased chickens shortly before he became ill. The case brings the total number of human infections with influenza A (H5N1) since December 2003 to 117.

WHO confirms the presence of the H5N1 virus in Romania on 13th October and reiterates that The WHO level of pandemic alert remains unchanged at phase 3: a virus new to humans is causing infections, but does not spread easily from one person to another.

The Ministry of Public Health in Thailand confirms its first case of human infection with H5N1 avian influenza since 08 October 2004. A 48-year old man developed symptoms on 13 October, was hospitalized, but died less than a week later. Authorities linked his infection to close contact with diseased poultry.

The Ministry of Health in Indonesia confirms two additional cases of human infection with H5N1 avian influenza. The first, a four-year-old boy from Sumatra Island in Lampung Province, developed symptoms on 4 October and recovered. Though the boy was a nephew of a 21-year-old man from Lampung reported infected on 10 October 2005 who lived in the same village, human-to-human transmission is considered unlikely.

The second confirmed case was a 23-year-old man from West Java, who died on 30 September.

November 2005

Officials in Thailand confirm two non-fatal cases of the disease: an 18-month-old boy and a 50-year-old woman from Bangkok.

The Ministry of Health in Indonesia confirms another non-fatal human infection with the case of a 16-year-old boy who developed symptoms of fever followed by breathing difficulties. A further fatal two cases in Indonesia, a 16-year-old girl and 20-year-old woman from Jakarta bring the total newly confirmed cases total to 12, 7 of which were fatal.

Surveillance for human cases in China intensifies following a recurrence of H5N1 in poultry, with officials reporting 25 fresh outbreaks in poultry in nine provinces.

China confirms the country's first two human cases of bird flu and investigates the possibility of human-to-human transmission. A 24-year-old female from the Anhui Province becomes the country's first fatality and a 9-year-old boy is hospitalized with respiratory symptoms but recovers.

The boy's 12-year-old sister was hospitalized in October and died the following day of severe bilateral pneumonia and acute respiratory distress syndrome. According to WHO, samples from the girl are inadequate for testing and the exact cause of death will probably never be known (WHO reports only laboratory-confirmed cases).

The Chinese Ministry of Health and WHO participate in a joint mission to the Anhui Province of the country to investigate two fatal cases of H5N1 infection that occurred in female farmers aged 24 and 35 years.

A newly confirmed fatal case in Viet Nam coincides with a recurrence of outbreaks in poultry. The Ministry of Health later confirms a further non-fatal case: a 15-year-old boy from Hai Phong Province who recovered after treatment in hospital. Viet Nam has reported 66 cases (22 fatal) since December 2004.

December 2005

A 41-year-old woman from the south-eastern province of Fujian dies on 21 December, China's seventh laboratory-confirmed case and third fatality. To date, China has reported human cases in six provinces and regions: Hunan, Anhui, Guangxi, Liaoning, Jiangxi and Fujian.

The first case occurred in an 8-year-old boy from Central Jakarta. He developed symptoms of fever and cough on 8 December. He was hospitalized on 13 December, and died on 15 December.

The second case occurred in a 39-year-old man from East Jakarta. He first reported symptoms of fever, headache, cough and shortness of breath on 9 December. He was hospitalized on 11 December and died on 12 December.

These newly confirmed cases bring the total number in Indonesia to 16. Of these cases, 11 were fatal.

Realizing that this was an actual case study of pandemic level viral infection that altered its course and mutated itself ultimately in to a strain that killed 1/3 of infected persons.

Looking at the data, one can demonstrably view the global outbreak and how it affected those infected with the virus. An eventual zombie outbreak is not that far of a leap when it comes to infectious diseases and their growth globally.

This is where your survival skills and your preparedness will come into play. Being ready at the slightest sign or provocation of an impending bioterrorist attack. Whether it be of the zombie kind or that of a mild flu.

Combating the evil undead and protecting what you have earned and made with your own sweat equity. These will be your own defining moments in the new coming collapse of society and the beginning of a global emergency. As the creeping dead fill the planet and eat their way through cities and towns only to emerge in your very own neighborhood.

Now as a final note, there are no undead zombies that we currently know of. There have been no recent reports of walking dead strolling through the streets consuming a terrorized public. There are no news agencies reporting on strange behaviors of human attacks led by a band of gluttonous brain feasting soulless automatons. So, for the time being, we are safe and sound. This is our time to prepare for an emergency. This will be our allowance to ready ourselves for any impending doomsday scenario that may come our way.

We can still take solace in understanding that even if we never see a zombie attack we will still have the proper training and insight that will save ourselves and our families' distress in any such catastrophe as a hurricane, flood, earthquake or geological disaster that may occur.

We have been using this guide to teach and educate the reader in a humorous and light-hearted method the needed set of proficiencies to accomplish the human goals of competent survival in any given situation. Knowing that with experience and readiness you will have the aptitude to accomplish anything you set your mind to.

If this resource has been able to qualify your know how to better comprehend the necessity to prepare and acknowledge that disasters happen and that we can only prep for such events in advance and deal with the realities of a natural misadventure.

Learning the myriad of life skills that can propel us to not only survive a fallout from nature's wrath and bluster is the catalyst that will expand our efforts to build a new beginning. Under any circumstances, the readiness will benefit what we know to grow our lives from mere survival to an exponential understanding of resources and how to utilize them properly. Ultimately learning that we don't just survive but overcome and adapt to our surroundings and flourish where others may fail.

If you fail in the zombie apocalypse it will mean you probably got eaten. Your troubles will be over so there is still no need to worry.

www.ingramcontent.com/pod-product-compliance
Lightning Source LLC
Chambersburg PA
CBHW072242260726
48657CB00001BA/26